ideas number twenty-five
ideas number twenty-six
ideas number twenty-seven
ideas number twenty-eight

Four Complete Volumes of Ideas in One

Edited by Wayne Rice and Mike Yaconelli.
Previously published as four separate books.

Your Idea May Be Worth $100

It's worth at least $25 if we publish it in a future volume of **Ideas**. And it's worth $100 if it's chosen as the outstanding idea of the book it appears in.

It's not really a contest, though—just our way of saying thanks for sharing your creativity with us. If you have a good idea that worked well with your group, send it in. We'll look it over and decide whether or not we can include it in a future **Ideas** book. If we do, we'll send you at least 25 bucks!

In addition to that, the **Ideas** editor will select one especially creative idea from each new book as the outstanding idea of that particular book—and send a check for $100 to its contributor.

So don't let your good ideas go to waste. Write them down and send them to us, accompanied by this form. Expain your ideas completely (without getting ridiculous) and include illustrations, diagrams, photos, samples, or any other materials you think are helpful.

FILL OUT BELOW

Name_____

Address _____

City _____State ___ Zip _____

Phone (_____)_____

I hereby submit the attached idea(s) to Youth Specialties for publication in **Ideas** and guarantee that, to my knowledge, the publication of these ideas by Youth Specialties does not violate any copyright belonging to another party. I understand that, if accepted for publication in **Ideas**, the idea(s) becomes the property of Youth Specialties. I also understand that I will receive payment for these ideas, the exact amount to be determined by Youth Specialties, payable upon acceptance.

Signature _____

Write or type your idea(s) (one idea per sheet) and attach it to this form or to a copy of this form. Include your name and address with each idea you send. Mail to **Ideas**, 1224 Greenfield Drive, El Cajon, CA 92021. Ideas submitted to Youth Specialties cannot be returned.

ISBN 0-910125-31-7 (Ideas Combo 25–28)

ISBN 0-910125-00-7 (Ideas Complete Library, Volumes 1–52)

© Copyright 1980, 1981, 1983, 1985 by Youth Specialties

1224 Greenfield Drive, El Cajon, Ca 92021

619/440-2333

Ideas in this book have been voluntarily submitted by individuals and groups who claim to have used them in one form or another with their youth groups. Before you use an idea, evaluate it for its suitability to your own groups, for any potential risks, for safety precautions that must be taken, and for advance preparation that may be required. Youth Specialties, Inc., is not responsible for, nor has it any control over, the use or misuse of any of the ideas published in this book.

table of contents

CHAPTER FOUR: SPECIAL EVENTS 142

CHAPTER FIVE: YOUTH GROUP LEADERSHIP 159

CHAPTER SIX: FUND RAISERS 164

CHAPTER SEVEN: PUBLICITY 168

CHAPTER EIGHT: CAMPING. 180

CHAPTER NINE: FAMILY MINISTRY 194

Chapter One

Crowd Breakers

ABDUL THE MAGNIFICENT

This is a mind reading stunt which, when done right, is downright spooky. Give each person a slip of paper and ask them to write a short sentence on it. The slips are then folded, collected, and "Abdul" (who can be dressed appropriately) proceeds to perform the task of reading the sentences to the group without opening the papers.

How is it done? Abdul also puts one slip of paper in the box along with the others, only he puts some kind of identifying mark on his. When the reading starts, he picks one of the slips from the box, rubs it on his forehead without opening it, and offers any sentence as a guess as to what is on the paper. He then looks at the paper, and to his dismay he is wrong, but that will soon be forgotten. He can blame it on the fact that the "spirits" aren't quite right yet, but that the next one should be better. It's important not to dwell on this mistake long. Just get on with the next one. It's also important not to reveal what was actually on the paper guessed incorrectly. Just get rid of it and go on. Another slip of paper is held to the forehead, and Abdul then repeats the sentence which was actually on the previous paper. After rubbing his forehead, he opens this second slip of paper, confirms that he is correct, and asks the person who wrote that sentence to identify it. Everyone is impressed. Another paper is drawn and again, Abdul repeats the sentence that was on the previously opened slip. Each time he opens up a slip of paper to see if he is "correct", he is actually learning the next sentence. The important thing is to stay one slip ahead. When he comes to his own slip, which has been held until last, he repeats the sentence on the previous slip, and that takes care of all of them. If this is done smoothly, it will really baffle the group. (Contributed by Mike Andujar, Los Gatos, California)

ADD-A-LETTER

This game works best with a group of 15 or less. Have the group sit in a circle. One person begins to spell a word, giving a letter. The next person adds another letter, each person attempting to add a letter *without* completing a word. A person gets a "mark" against him (you can possibly mark on their hand with a marker of some kind) whenever he accidentally finishes a word or is forced to say the last letter in a word. A person is out of the game when he gets five "marks." A person can fake a letter when it seems he is forced to finish a word. If the next person thinks he is faking, and doesn't have a word in mind, he can "challenge." If he catches the person who is bluffing, the bluffer gets a mark. If the person challenged can give the word he had in mind, then the challenger gets a mark. The winner is the last person left in the game. All words must be legitimate words, verifiable in a complete dictionary. (Contributed by Brian Schoeffler, Bath, New York)

BANG, YOU'RE DEAD

This is a game in which the leader knows the "secret" and the rest of the group is to try and guess how it's done. Everyone should be seated around the room in a casual manner, with the leader at the front. After everyone is quiet, the leader raises his hand and points it like a gun, and says "Bang, you're dead." He then asks the group to guess who he shot. It's hardly ever the person who was being pointed at. Several people will guess, and they will most likely be wrong. Then you announce who it was that you actually shot.

You do it several times, changing what you do each time to throw people off, but each time pointing a finger at someone and saying, "Bang, you're dead!" People try to guess, and then you announce who it really was. Make sure thay they understand that it is possible to know right away who it is that had been shot, but they have to figure out what the "secret" or "clue" is.

And just what is the secret? The person who was actually shot is the first person to speak after you say "Bang, you're dead." Sooner or later, someone will catch on as you perhaps make it a little more obvious, and that only baffles the rest of the group even more. It's fun as well as frustrating. (Contributed by Tim Spilker, Lakeside, California)

BITE THE ONION

This a "Truth or Consequences" type of game in which everyone sits around in a circle. Begin by passing around an onion, "hot potato" style, and after a short while the group leader yells, "Stop!" The person who last touched the onion before the "Stop," is given the onion (if he/she doesn't already have it). The person who passed the onion to the last person may ask that person any question on any subject. The person with the onion has the choice whether or not to answer the question, but if he refuses to answer the question, he must take a bite out of the onion. The

onion then gets passed around for another round.

Although this is a fun game, remember to initially allow participants the option to "pass." For those who wish not to play, you might want to provide an alternative game for those people. But usually everyone wants to play, and there are only a few voluntary bites taken from the onion. Be sure to have a camera ready to catch facial expressions when someone does bite the onion. It's a lot of fun. (Contributed by Malcolm McQueen, San Anselmo, California)

THE BUCK STOPS HERE

Here's a stunt that almost everyone has to try. Place a dollar bill on the ground and challenge the kids in your group that anyone who can jump over the dollar bill lengthwise gets to keep the dollar.

There is a catch, however. Before they jump over the bill, they must grab their toes (or both feet), holding on to the front of their feet, and not let go while they jump over the dollar bill. You might also want to mention these rules:

1. You must jump forward over the bill.
2. If you fall down in the process of jumping, you are disqualified.
3. Your heels must clear the vertical plane of the end of the bill after you jump in order to be successful.

Needless to say, it's impossible to do. You may want to try it yourself, however, before you risk your own money, or you may want to put two bills end to end to make it even more difficult. (Contributed by Tom Stanley, Chicago, Illinois)

CARTOON CREATIVITY

Cut a number of cartoons out of magazines and newspapers, remove the captions, and paste them on large sheets or paper with plenty of room at the bottom. Then hang them on the wall of your room and invite the youth group to view them at their leisure and make up their own captions. They should use their own creativity and write them in below the appropriate pictures. You could offer a prize to the best captions, or "prime the pump" by bringing in captions of your own ahead of time. It's a great way to keep the group occupied when they are just coming in, milling around, and waiting for things to get started. (Contributed by Melvin Schroer, Atascadero, California)

COMMON GROUND

This is a small group experience that is fun and that helps kids to get to know each other a lot better. The group is divided up into discussion groups of from five to seven per group, and then each group is given a sheet of instructions. The basic idea is for each group to come up with something that they *all* like or *all* dislike in a variety of categories (see list below). They are encouraged to be honest rather than just trying to "go for the points."

For each consensus reached, the group will receive a certain number of points (whatever you want). You could give ten points for any answer that everyone in the group had in common, and fewer points for answers that only some of the kids in the group had in common. For example, if only five out of the group of seven had a particular thing in common, then they would only get five points instead of the ten. Set a time limit of around ten minutes for this exercise.

Category	Like	Dislike
1. Food		
2. Game		
3. TV Show		
4. Gift received		
5. School subject		
6. Chore at home		
7. Song		
8. Hobby		
9. Way to spend Saturday		
10. Sport		

Next, the group is to come up with as many other shared experiences as they possibly can. They would receive additional points for each one of these. For example:

1. Got a B on last report card
2. Been sad over the death of a loved one
3. Been stood up by a friend
4. Went on a back-packing trip

Give the group five minutes to try and come up with as many of these common experiences as possible. Any experience is acceptable, so long as each person in the group has shared that experience. Someone in the group should act as secretary and write them down as they are named by the group and agreed to. At the end of the time limit, the group can total up its points.

This exercise is excellent for "breaking the ice" and helps kids to see just how much they have in common with each other. (Contributed by Syd Schnaars, Delaware, Ohio)

COMMUNITY QUIZ

This is a crowd breaker that works great as a mixer. It works best in situations when you know everyone who will be in attendance. You will need to contact each person in advance, get certain information from them, and then include that information in a written quiz that you print up before your meeting or event. The quiz should contain the same number of multiple choice or true-false questions as there are people (or you could have more than one question for each person).

You can then use the quiz in one of several ways. One way is to simply give everyone a copy of the quiz and they begin milling around the room asking each other for the information needed to answer the questions correctly. At the end of a time limit, whoever has the most correct answers wins. Another way would be to have everyone take the test first, and then have each person stand up and give the correct answer as you go down the list of questions. Either way works fine, although the first suggestion is more active and requires more group interaction. A combination of both would be to have everyone take the test first, and then mill around the room asking each person for the correct answers to see if they were right or wrong.

The key is to compose questions that are humorous and interesting and which include "little-known" facts about each person. It's not only fun, but very informative.

Some sample questions:

1. Danny Thompson is saving his money to buy:
   a. A Lear jet
   b. A hair transplant
   c. A moped
   d. A banjo

2. Lisa Burns hates:
   a. sardines
   b. artichokes
   c. cranberries
   d. Danny Thompson

3. Bill Florden's dad once appeared on the Johnny Carson show.
   a. True
   b. False

4. Next Christmas, Paula Lovik's family is going:
   a. to stay home
   b. to Aspen, Colorado
   c. to her grandmother's house in Memphis
   d. crazy

(Contributed by Tom Collins, St. Petersburg, Florida)

ENDLESS WORD

Have the group form a circle. The first person gives a word and then counts 1-2-3-4-5 at a moderate speed. Before this person says five, the person to their right has to say another word that begins with the last letter of the word just said. This continues on around the circle. It is counted as a miss if that person can't think of a word before the person before them says Five. Two misses and the person is out of the game. (Or one if you have a very large group.) If it is the person's first miss, he starts it again with any word. No one is allowed to repeat a word that has already been spoken. If no one is getting put out, have them count to five more rapidly. Or if everyone is getting out, have them count to ten or fifteen instead of five. This game is a lively one, and you'll soon find out who is out to "get" the person next to them. (Contributed by Brian Schoeffler, Bath, New York)

GUESS WHAT?

Here's a good game that can be used as a crowdbreaker at the beginning of an event while people are still arriving. You will need to do a little advance preparation by putting in various places around the room: a jar full of small balls or beans, a ribbon hanging from the ceiling, a display of photos of famous (or not so famous) people, a package that you have weighed in advance, a box with something in it, and an assortment of bottles with a different substance in each bottle which gives off an odor. Then give each person a game sheet like the one below.

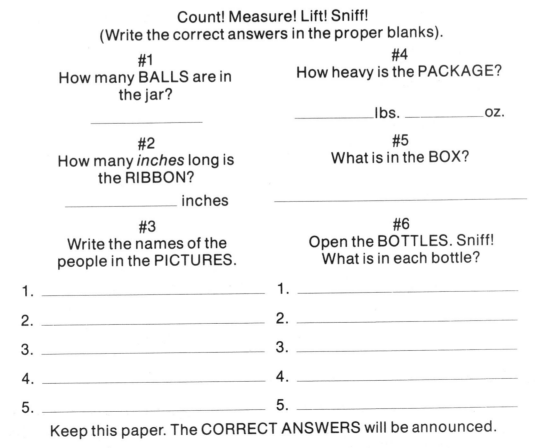

Count! Measure! Lift! Sniff!
(Write the correct answers in the proper blanks).

#1
How many BALLS are in the jar?

_____

#2
How many *inches* long is the RIBBON?

_____ inches

#3
Write the names of the people in the PICTURES.

1. _____
2. _____
3. _____
4. _____
5. _____

#4
How heavy is the PACKAGE?

_____lbs. _____oz.

#5
What is in the BOX?

_____

#6
Open the BOTTLES. Sniff!
What is in each bottle?

1. _____
2. _____
3. _____
4. _____
5. _____

Keep this paper. The CORRECT ANSWERS will be announced.

13

When everyone has had enough time to try to figure out the answers, have them exchange papers while you announce the correct answers. You might want to award a prize to whoever gets the most correct, or separate prizes to the winners in each of the various categories. (Contributed by Mrs. F. S. Richardett, Howell, New Jersey)

HALLOWEEN HYSTERIA

Here's a variation of the game "Confusion" which is great for Halloween. As with regular Confusion, everyone is given a sheet with the list below printed on it. They should also get a pencil. On go, everyone tries to complete the instructions in any order they wish. When they complete each one, they should have the other

1. Sneak up behind someone, tap their shoulder, and when they turn around, make a face and yell "BOO!" as loud as you can. They initial here _____.

2. Do your best impression of Count Dracula and say to someone: "I want to drink your blood." They initial here _____.

3. Get three people together and SCREAM together for five seconds. One person initials here _____.

4. Find someone with a funny costume and laugh at them for ten seconds while pointing at them. They initial here _____.

5. Go to someone with makeup on and howl like a wolf--three short howls and one long howl. They initial here _____.

6. Find someone who does not have a costume on and say to that person: "Hey, your outfit looks pretty cute!" They initial here _____.

7. Using your own address, tell someone where there is a "haunted house," and show them how to get there by drawing a map on the back of their sheet. They initial here _____.

8. Go to three people and for three long seconds, look like you just saw a ghost and then shout, "I did, I did, I did!" The third person initials here _____.

9. Walk around the room for one minute acting like you are the Great Pumpkin, telling everybody you walk by how much you weigh. Get the last person you tell to initial here _____.

10. Run around and around someone yelling "trick or treat," not letting that person do anything until they give you something (anything). They initial here _____.

person involved initial that particular item. The first to complete the entire list is the winner.

To organize the confusion, you might circle a different number (ahead of time) on each sheet. Then announce that the list must be completed in order, beginning with the number that is circled, then back to number 1 after number 10.

(Contributed by Jerry Pounds, Denver, Colorado)

MONTEZUMA'S MEMOS

This is a fun (and tasty) crowd breaker that works best with smaller groups. Buy a bag of "Mini-taco" corn chips at the grocery store. They look like Mexican fortune cookies. Then, make up small strips of paper that can be stuffed into the little mini-tacos. On each strip of paper, there is typed a message of some kind. You could put announcements of coming events, crazy stunts that have to be performed on the spot, Bible verses, or whatever. The little strips need to be stuffed into the chips in advance, put in a bowl, and then passed around to the group. Each person takes a turn opening up one of the chips (breaking it), and then reading the message to the group (and doing whatever it says to do, if applicable). Of course, the person may then go ahead and eat the chip.

To add a little excitement to this, you might put a strip of paper in one chip with the words "Montezuma's Revenge" on it. Whoever gets that one gets a penalty of some kind. (Contributed by Don Maddox, Long Beach, California)

MYSTERY BOOKS

The following story should be printed up (without the bold type) and given to each person. The object is to try and find the 39 books of the Bible that are hidden in the story. The solution is provided for you in bold type. For another game like this one, see "Hidden Books" in *IDEAS Number 11*.

While motoring in Palestine I met Chief Me**jud, ges**ticulating wildly. His f**ez, ra**iment, and features were odd. I never saw so dis**mal a Chi**ef. On **mark**et days he pum**ps alms** from everyone, **a mos**t common practice. A glance shows that he **acts** queerly. Excuse my spea**king s**o, but he was showing a crowd how they used to **revel at lon**iam bouts, when t**he brew s**eemed bad.

A fakir was seated o**n a hum**p, minus **hose a**nd shirt, and wearing as co**mic a h**at as they make. He pointed u**p eter**nally toward a rudely carved letter "**J**" **on a h**igh cliff that was unusually ste**ep**. "**He's**", I ans**w**ered, "absolutely right!"

My companion then cried: "See that '**J**'? **Oh, n**ow I know we are near the Ancient Ai. Is th**is Ai a h**oly place?" **From ans**wers given elsewhere, I'll say not! We asked the age of the big stone "**J**": "**O, el**even centuries at least."

I know that in such a **jam, es**cort was necessary. Besides, our car stuck in a **rut h**ere. So leaving the se**dan, I el**bowed nearer the fakir. A toothless **hag gai**ned access to his side, and paused to **rest her**self on a **mat. The w**oman hinted, "You have treasure?" To which I retorted: "Not **I! Moth, y**ou know, and rust corrupt earthly store!" Me**jud e**xpressed a wish to accompany us, but I decreed, "Thy party we will not ann**ex, O dus**ty Chief! I am tracing a cargo of lost to-bacco. That's my **job**!" To the chief's expression of sorrow over the toba**cco loss I ans**wered, "It would all have gone up in smoke anyway."

My brother is a tram**p (rover), B.S.**, from Harvard, too. His name is Eu**gene. Sis**ter is nursing him now. He is still a member of Gamma **Phi. Lemon**ade is his favorite drink when he is ill. They asked, "Where is the prodi**gal at**?" **I ans**wered tha**t it us**ed to be incorrect to use "at" that way, but that the **flu ke**pt Eugene at home this year. It really is to**o bad, I, a h**ome body, roaming the Orient, and he, a tramp at home in bed.

(Contributed by Bryan Schoeffler, Bath, New York)

MYSTERY NAMES

This is just like "Mystery Books" only the story here contains over eighty Bible names rather than books of the Bible. The story doesn't make much sense, but it does include a river, a town, an island, a capital, a large city in Egypt, a valley, a country, a continent, and not less than seventy-seven men and women. Print up the story ("The Rambler"), excluding the underlining, and have your group try to find as many names as possible within a given time limit. They can work individually, or in teams. You might want to give them a couple of "free" names just to get them started. Tell them to ignore punctuation marks when looking for the names. The answers are underlined here for your convenience.

THE RAMBLER

Major Dan, I Elucidate, sang a solo monotonously to the viola banjo's ephemeral strains. "A rare hobo am I," sang he, "who seeks the fount of elixir of life. I must shun the place where toxic ale begins to flow." Said he, "I find it a bit hard; I see not a chance for a job. For me this crisis era brings hope, terror, and despair alternately. Diamonds are the lot of some, but fate refuseth me such things. I have only my banjo. Abner and Diana, both so well-robed and fed, refuse to help me. In some hotel I shall seek what refresheth, Ham and Jam especially. In cakes there is delight. I long ago as a pupil ate many in a single visit. Why should this catastrophe be to me? Singing a solo is of no profit. In Indiana a man could find employment and a habitation, at least such a man as I."

So he rode a freight train to Henry's house. On the doorstep Henry had a huge, hazily figured mat. The work of hemming it was done by his wife. "Suzanna, omit this hem," said Dan; "one hem I, a handy man, could do evenly if it were well marked out. This way it makes a united pattern."

Henry was hurrying to bring from the barn a basket of eggs. Tho massive and strong he was a ruthless, parsimonious, and avid man with a grip particularly strong. He grabs a lombardy poplar club, and, as a male knave, put it uselessly down again on the concrete walk, and stood agog when he saw who it was. Dan with candor casually remarked, "Your wrath ensues because I am ostensibly a stranger. As I approached I did not mean to mar your peace of mind, or mar that smile of Susanna's. I surely do look rakish; just usual, however." Then playing the banjo as he rose, he stood there and sang adeptly.

"I think the banjo elegant," said Susanna thankfully, and she bade him play and sing. He sang a chorus, then a racy Russian folk song, then an Aramaic ballad. He had found friends; and now a big ailment, homesickness, was gone.

(Contributed by Bryan Schoeffler, Bath, New York)

NAME THAT HYMN

Put together a "rhythm band" with wooden blocks, moroccas, bells, sticks, and so forth. Have the band practice some well known hymns using only those instruments. Then divide the audience into teams and have a contest to see which team can guess the hymns as they are played by the rhythm band. It's not easy trying to guess "A Mighty Fortress Is Our God" played on a bike horn or "Away In A Manger" done expertly on sandpaper blocks. (Contributed by Don Maddox, Monrovia, California)

THE PANTS GAME

Assuming that most everyone wears pants, here's a game that you can use almost anytime. Give everyone a score sheet and a pencil, and as you go down the following list, have them award themselves 10 point for:

Each pocket
Each belt loop
If you're wearing a belt
If the belt is brown
If the buckle on the belt is silver
If there's a Levi tag somewhere on the pants
If there's ornamental stitching on the pockets
If there are cuffs
If the hems are frayed
If there's a grease spot or stain
If there's a patch
If there's gold or yellow top stitching
If there is elastic in the waist
If there is a wallet in your pocket
If there is a hole in your pants somewhere
If your pants are any color besides blue
If your pants are long enough to touch the floor

You can add other things if you wish, possibly including other items of clothing as well. The person who has the highest total number of points is the winner. An appropriate prize might be a patch or an old pair of discarded pants. (Contributed by Nancy Cheatham, Olathe, Kansas)

PINCHY-WINCHY

This is a stunt which is set up as a game—boys against girls. The best way to do this would be to have three couples volunteer to compete. Each couple is brought up one at a time to play the game. They boy faces the girl and must first grab the girl's cheek with his thumb and forefinger and say "pinchy-winchy" while making faces or whatever. The idea is to try to make the girl laugh. If the boy is successful, he gets one point, and if he is unsuccessful, the girl gets one point. Then the girl gets to pinch the boy's cheek and she also says "pinchy-winchy" and makes a face or does anything she wants to try and make the boy laugh without touching him again. After three tries on each side, the next couple does it, and then the last couple.

By now, the last couple is really going to give it all they've got and score big. At least that's what the boy thinks. The girl has armed herself, without the boy's knowledge, with a tube of lipstick which she holds behind her back. Every time she pinches the boy's cheek she puts a little lipstick on her fingers and rubs the lipstick on the boy's face. The boy never realizes what's going on till it's too late, allowing his face to literally be painted, and the audience just loves it. (Contributed by Glenn Davis, Winston-Salem, North Carolina)

PORTRAIT CONTEST

Give each person a couple sheets of art paper and some charcoal or felt-tip pens for drawing. Then have the kids pair off and draw each other's portrait. Give the kids about 20 to 30 minutes to work on these. These portraits should be only from the shoulders up.

After the portraits are finished, they should all be numbered and should have the name of the person drawn on the back of the portrait. Then they should all be hung up on the wall. All of the kids then go around, look at the portraits, and try to guess who the portraits are. A prize can be awarded either to the one who drew the portrait of which got the most correct guesses, or to the one who guesses the most names right, or the kids can vote on the best portrait, and so on. It's a lot of fun, and it's great as a mixer, especially if the people do not know each other very well. (Contributed by Kim Swenson, Stanchfield, Minnesota)

SACK SIGN-UP

Here's a good idea for a mixer or a quick get-acquainted game. Give every person a small paper sack which they must place over their right hand. They also receive a pen or pencil. When the game starts, everyone must go around the room and get signatures on their paper sack, writing with their left hand. All of

those who are left-handed should put the paper sack over their left hand and write with their right hand. The first person who obtains signatures from everyone in the room is the winner, or for larger groups, the first person to get a certain number of signatures (like 20) is the winner. (Contributed by Julie Von Vett, Minneapolis, Minnesota)

SCRAMBLED NAME

Here's a little game which works well as a mixer when groups are larger (15 or more) and when people don't know each other. Everyone gets a piece of paper and pencil, and writes their name down with the letters all mixed up. In other words, if your name is Harvey Furd, then you might write it as "Vreahy Urfd."

Then all the names are put in a hat and each person draws a piece of paper. On go, everyone is to try and unscramble the name on the piece of paper they drew. They may figure it out by themselves or they can seek help from others. Once they know the name of the person, they must seek that person out—either by shouting out the person's name or by going around asking their name. Once they find the person, they must have the person sign their name on a piece of paper.

The game can continue until a time limit is up, or until everyone has figured out all the names. (Contributed by Bob Bilanski, Astoria, Oregon)

SMELL THE BROOM

Two people need to know how this game works. One of them can brag to the audience about his keen sense of smell. To prove this a broom is brought in and given to the other person to hold parallel to the floor in both hands. The bragger leaves the room while the broom holder asks someone from the audience to

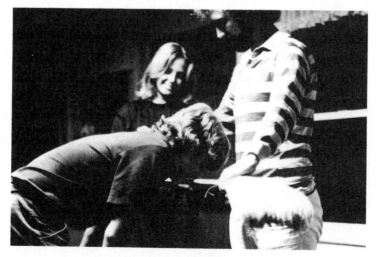

touch the broom handle anyplace he/she chooses. When this is done the person who left the room is called back in to smell back and forth across the broom handle to "smell out" the spot where the person touched it. The person who is doing the smelling does so by moving his nose across the handle while looking at the holder's feet. The holder should have shoes on. When the smeller's nose crosses the spot where the broom was touched the holder moves his toes on one foot up and down very slightly to indicate to the smeller his nose just crossed the spot which was touched. The smeller now knowing where the spot is can point to it and ask if the audience wants to try again. A lot of fun can be had with this game since the movement of the shoe is so slight the audience cannot detect it. (Contributed by John W. Fritsche, Jacksonville, Illinois)

THANKSGIVING BINGO

Here's a mixer that works well at Thanksgiving. Simply print up a bingo card, like the one illustrated below. Fill in each of the blanks with something that the kids in your group would probably be thankful for. Make some of them very general, like

A GOOD SINGING VOICE	MY NEW CAR	MY OWN ROOM	A CLOSE FAMILY	GOOD LOOKS
MY 16th BIRTHDAY THIS YEAR	MY STEREO	AN ANSWERED PRAYER	GOOD HEALTH ALL YEAR	MY JOB
NO ZITS	SOMEONE WHO LOVES ME	A SUCCESSFUL DIET TO LOSE WEIGHT	A FUN VACATION LAST SUMMER	GETTING TO GO SKIING LAST YEAR
MAKING THE TEAM	A FRIEND WHO BECAME A CHRISTIAN	GOOD GRADES	WINNING AN AWARD LAST YEAR	A NEW BABY IN THE FAMILY
A BIG BILL PAID OFF LAST YEAR	A BIG PROBLEM RECENTLY SOLVED	FINDING A NEW FRIEND RECENTLY	MY GUITAR PLAYING ABILITY	NOT FALLING ASLEEP DURING THE SERMON

"Someone to Love" and others that are more specific like "Making the Football Team." The idea is for everyone to go around the room and to find people who are thankful for particular items. If you get five in a row, up, down, or diagonally, then you are a winner. Play until everyone has five in a row, and then perhaps each person can share their bingo combination. Encourage each person to not only sign a person's bingo card, but to also elaborate on why they are thankful for that particular item. Another rule is that no person may write their name twice on anyone's bingo card. Only one square per person. This game can be used with adults as well, simply by changing the categories to things like "My Successful Operation," "My New Granddaughter," "Buying a New Home," and so forth. (Contributed by Dave Sauder, Corning, California)

TOP 40

This is a fun guessing game that can be used as a quick crowdbreaker. Tape-record bits and pieces of some of the top 40 hits of the month, week, or whatever onto a cassette. You can usually accomplish this by recording them right off of the radio. Edit it so that only a second or two of each song can be heard. Then when you play it back for the kids, see how many of them can identify all of the songs. Usually kids are so familiar with these songs, that it is nearly impossible to stump anyone, even when you only play one second of each song. This would be a good opener for a meeting that includes a discussion on rock music or a similar topic. (Contributed by Richard Mallyon, Thousand Oaks, California)

WHAT'S THE MEANING, PART TWO

Here are some more "brain teasers" that are a lot of fun for kids to try and figure out. One group printed these up and titled it "University of Poland Entrance Exam." The object, of course, is to look at the arrangement of letters, and to write a word or phrase that interprets each one. For more, see "What's the Meaning" in *IDEAS Number Seventeen*.

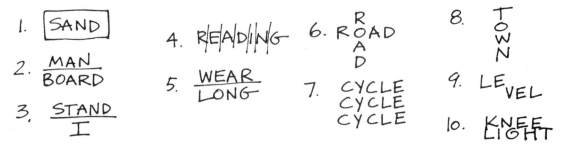

11. CHAIR

12. DICE
    DICE

13. T
   O
   U
   C
   H

14. GROUND
    FEET
    FEET
    FEET
    FEET
    FEET
    FEET

15. $\dfrac{MIND}{MATTER}$

16. HE'S/HIMSELF

17. ECNALG

18.

19. ✝✝

20. K
    C
    E
    H
    C

21. O—144

22. OFF
    OFF

23. SIDE/SIDE

24. KY O UO
         L
         O

25. DOCTOR
    DOCTOR

26. DATE
    DATE

(Contributed by J. Russell Matzke, Colorado Springs, Colorado, and Mary Highlander, Stone Mountain, Georgia)

Chapter Two

Games

AIR RAID

Next time you are playing games, announce at the beginning that the group is always in danger of an air attack from enemies of unknown origin. If the words "Air Raid" are shouted out by the leader, everyone would be well advised to fall flat on the floor. The last person to do so will be penalized a substantital number of points from their team score.

The element of surprise works best with this. Every so often during the regular games, the leader should just yell out "Air Raid!" There are always a few kids who forget and are left standing, thus costing their team some valuable points. It's a great little "extra added attraction" to a recreation time. (Contributed by Joe Falkner, Fort Worth, Texas)

ANIMAL RUMMY

Here's a good game for parties and such where you don't want much physical activity, but you want to have some fun. Give everybody a piece of paper and a pencil. Then have each person write someone's name at the top of a sheet of paper, each letter to head up a column, like so:

H	U	B	E	R	T

Everyone should use the same name. The leader now calls "Animal" and each player writes the names of as many animals as he can in each column—the names being required to begin with the letter heading that particular column. Set a time limit and have everyone work on this till the time limit (2 minutes is usually plenty of time) is up. After they have finished the leader should ask for all the animals listed in the column and make a master list. Players receive points for each animal they have listed on their own sheet, plus each animal is given a bonus point value based on the number of players who did not have that particular animal listed.

This game can also be played with flowers, vegetables, trees, or cities or any other category that the leader can think up. It's a lot of fun. (Contributed by J. Russell Matzke, Colorado Springs, Colorado)

BADMINTON VOLLEYBALL

Here is another version of volleyball that works well in groups from 6 to 40. Have each person bring a badminton racquet to the game. In case there are those who do not have badminton racquets, you might have to provide a few extra, just in case. Even if you have to buy them, they are not very expensive. You'll also need a couple of "birdies" (shuttlecocks). Divide into two

teams and play badminton over a volleyball net, using regular volleyball rules. This can really be a riot with 15-20 kids on each side of the net with badminton racquets. For mixed groups, you might have all the guys play wrong-handed. (Contributed by John Marchak, Mooreland, Indiana)

BALANCING BRONCOS

Divide your group into two or more teams. The guys are the horses and the girls are the riders. The object of the game is for a girl to sit cross-legged (Indian-style) on the boy's back. He must go around an obstacle and back without her falling off. If she falls off they must start again at either the beginning or back to the half-way point. The girls can't hang on. They must try to balance. It is easier if they face backwards. If after you divide into teams you have more guys than girls, then the game is over when one team has sent all its guys around the obstacle. (You'll have to use some girls twice.) If the ratio is the other way, then all the girls have to ride. (You'll have to use some boys more than once.) This game moves quickly and is a lot harder than it sounds! (Contributed by Andy Strachan, Keithville, Louisiana)

BALLOON DROP RELAY

All you need are 40 or more inflated balloons (round ones), two or more teams made up of couples; each with a "dropper" (person who drops balloons), standing on a folding chair. Place the balloons in a box, line up the teams and you're ready to go.

The idea is to get the balloon to the other end in the fastest time. Before you start, the dropper positions him/herself up on the chair with the balloon ready to drop to the floor. The couples sit on the floor in front of the dropper, back to back, leaving enough room for the balloon to slip down between their backs. The couple then carefully stands, keeping the balloon between their backs and shuffles their way to the other end. Upon arrival the next balloon is dropped to the next couple, and so on until the entire team reaches the other side. If the balloon should burst or fall to the floor before reaching the finish line, the couple must return and start over. The dropper may drop as many balloons as needed, in order to get one positioned just where the couple wants it. No hands may be used at any time by the couples. This relay game is just as much fun to watch as it is to play!

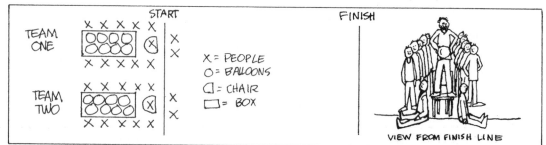

(Contributed by Tom Bougher, Mobile, Alabama)

BALLOON PIN THROW

Here's a crazy little game which can involve as few as four people, or it can be used for larger groups in a relay style. Each team has one of its members sit down in a chair, wearing a hat that has a stick pin or some kind of pin attached to the front of it. This would work best by rigging up a baseball cap with a straight pin taped onto the front of it and sticking out a little bit. If this is done as a relay, each person on the team has a balloon with a piece of string tied to it, and stands a short distance from the person who is seated in the chair wearing the hat. Each person then tries to toss their balloon toward the hat, so that the pin will pop their balloon. They hold on to the piece of string so that they can retrieve the balloon if they miss the pin. As soon as the balloon pops, they let the next person do it, and so on until everyone on the team has popped their balloon. You might test this a few times before you play it so that you can determine the proper distance for the foul line to be from the chair. It should be a challenge to accomplish, but not impossible. (Contributed by Ira Pacheco, Rialto, California)

BANANA WHISTLE

Divide group into three or more teams. Position three people from each team about 20 feet apart as shown in this diagram:

```
   X              X              X

          X              X              X
  Team 1         Team 2         Team 3

 X              X              X

Starting Line
```

27

A fourth person from each team goes to the starting line and is blindfolded. At a signal, the people positioned on the playing field begin to yell at the blindfolded person trying to get him to come toward them until they can touch him without moving from their positions. This must be done in order (player #1 first, then #2 and #3). At that point the blindfold is removed and the person runs back to the starting line where a fifth person is waiting to feed him a banana. As soon as possible after eating the banana he must whistle an assigned tune as loud as he can for at least 15 seconds. This is good for a lot of laughs and team competition. If there are more people on each team, you can have more than three on the playing field, or they always come in handy for cheering the person on. (Contributed by Brenda Clowers, Bethany, Oklahoma)

BEN HUR

This game is similar to the old "Blanket Race" or the "Chariot Race," but this one adds more speed and excitement. To begin with, chariots must be constructed from a burlap sack, two strips of wood (each 1/4" thick, 1-1/2" wide, and as long as the sack is wide), and eight pieces of rope or twine about 12-15 feet long. The two wood pieces are nailed together opposite each other on one end of the sack. Make sure the sack is held securely by the two pieces of wood. Drill four holes equally spaced and each large enough to allow two pieces of rope to be put through the holes as the harnesses.

Four people are then used as "horses," each using two ropes, one for each shoulder. A smaller person works best as the

chariot driver. The driver sits on the burlap sack and hangs on while the horses pull. Set up a single pole at the far end of an open field, find an "Empress" to drop the hanky, and the excitement starts. More chariots competing at one time will add greatly to the fun. It is also best to play this game on a soft grassy field, where there are no rocks or other obstacles. (Contributed by Alan Overland, Sturgeon Lake, Minnesota)

BERSERK

Here is a unique game that requires little skill, includes any amount of people and is 100% active. The object is for a group of any size to keep an equal amount of assigned tennis balls moving about a gymnasium floor until six penalties have been indicated.

The vocabulary for this game is unique and essential to the success of the game. It goes like this:

Rabid Nugget: a moving tennis ball
Hectic: a stationary tennis ball
Berserk: a referee's scream, designating a penalty
Frenzy: an elapsed time period measuring six Berserks
Logic: a tennis ball that becomes lodged unintentionally on or behind something
Illogic: a tennis ball that is craftilly stuck on or behind something
Paranoia: a player's feeling that the refs are picking on her/him

If thirty players are on the gym floor, thirty *Rabid Nuggets* are thrown, rolled, or bounced simultaneously onto the floor by one of the refs. There are three refs; one at each end of the court and one off to the side at mid-court. It is the duty of the two refs on the floor to try and spot *Hectics* and to generate a hysterical scream (a *Berserk*) so that all will recognize a penalty. The group has five seconds to start a *Hectic* moving again or another full throated *Berserk* is issued. The Berserking ref must point condemningly at the *Hectic* until it is again provided impetus.

Every fifteen seconds after a start the side line ref puts an additional *Rabid Nugget* into play until the final *Berserk* has been recorded.

The team is allowed six *Berserks,* at which juncture the ref on the sidelines, who is responsible for timing this melee, jumps up and down waving his arms yelling STOP—STOP—STOP.

The object is to keep the *Rabid Nuggets* moving as long as possible before six *Berserks* have been recorded. This time span is called a *Frenzy.* After a *Frenzy* ask the group to develop a strategy in order to keep the *Rabid Nuggets* moving for a longer span of time, i.e. increasing the *Frenzy.*

Other Rules:

1. A rabid nugget must be kicked (only kicked) randomly or to another player. It may not be held underfoot and simply moved back and forth.
2. If a rabid nugget becomes a logic or illogic, the ref must get the nugget back into motion. An illogic receives an immediate Berserk.

3. Official tennis balls are not essential to active and satisfying play. You could probably have a heck of a good game if everyone brought their own piece of Silly Putty.
4. There are no official time outs except for double loss of contact lenses or the misfortune of a fractured hang nail.

(Contributed by Karl Rohnke, Ipswich, Massachusetts)

BIBLE BROOM TWIST

Here's a game which combines a Bible quiz with a wild relay race. Divide the group into teams, with the same number of people on each team. The teams should then split in half with each half of the team on opposite ends of the playing area. (See diagram) In the center of the playing field there should be a broom for each team. There should also be a chair at the starting place for each of the teams.

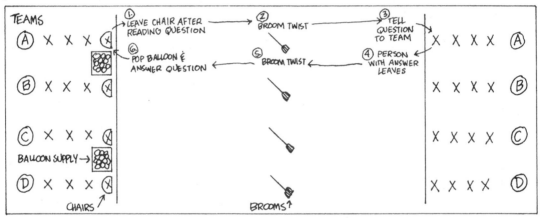

To begin the game, one person on each team sits in the chair. The leader gives to each seated person a slip of paper that has a question on it. They are not allowed to look at the question until the whistle blows. When the whistle is blown, the seated players read the question, leaves the question on the chair, and then runs towards the other half of their team on the other side of the playing area. When they reach the broom they must pick up the broom, hold it against their chest in a vertical manner, look up at the top of the broom, and make ten revolutions. They then drop the broom and run the rest of the way to their destination. When they reach the other half of their team, they announce the questions to their teammates. As a group, the team members try to come up with the right answer. As soon as they do, they send the first person in line back to the original side of the field, with the person again picking up the broom and turning around ten times while looking at the broom.

When the person with the answer reaches the chair, a blown up balloon will be on the chair. He must then sit on the chair, pop the balloon and then announce the correct answer to the question. If the leader determines that the answer is incorrect, that person must then run back to the other half of the team again, repeating the broom twist in the middle and try to come up with the correct answer. If the answer is correct, the team wins an appropriate number of points. There should be as many questions as there are team members on each side of the playing area.

This could also be good in a simplified fashion by having the entire team at the same end of the field. The questions would then be shouted to all the teams and as soon as the team had the correct answer, their first person in line would then run out to the middle, do the broom twist, run back to the team, pop the balloon and give the answer. (Contributed by Matthew S. McFadden, Lexington, Kentucky)

BIBLE FAMILY FEUD

Survey your adult Sunday School class to get their answers to the questions listed below. On the surveys, people are asked to give one answer per question. Then compile your "survey results," rank-ordering all the answers from most to least common, and use these results in a game of "Family Feud" patterned after the popular TV show. It's easiest if you play for games rather than points, like they do on TV. Each team sends a player to the front. The question is asked of these two players. The player giving the most common response has the option of playing the game or passing it to the player of the other team. The team that plays the game must name all the responses given (or a maximum of the top six responses) without making three mistakes. If they do, they are the winning team. If not, the other team has a chance to "steal" the game if they can name a correct response not named by the other team. The team winning the most games, or best two out of three, etc., is the winner.

Possible Questions:
1. Name a disciple of Jesus.
2. Name one of the Ten Commandments.
3. Name a parable of Jesus.
4. Name a city in Israel.
5. Name a miracle of Jesus.
6. Name one of the fruits of the Spirit.
7. Name one of Paul's letters.
8. Name one of the plaques of Egypt.
9. Name a famous Old Testament character.
10. Name a famous New Testament character.

(Contributed by Ron Elliott, Bloomington, Minnesota)

BIRDS HAVE FEATHERS

This is a fun variation of "Simon Says." One player leads. The others flap their arms flying back when the leader names something with feathers. When the players flap their wings on the calling of something that doesn't have feathers, he drops out. The leader may flap his wings anytime to confuse the others. He makes his calls rapidly. For example: "Birds have feathers, Geese have feathers. Ducks have feathers. Frogs have feathers. Goats have feathers. Sparrows have feathers. Swans have feathers. Dogs have feathers." (Contributed by Russell Matzke, Colorado Springs, Colorado)

BLACK OUT

Here's a new twist to musical chairs that is a real riot. First arrange the chairs in a circle facing outward. Players form a circle around the outside of the chairs. Explain that players must keep their hands behind their backs. Also explain that the boys must walk around the chairs clock-wise and the girls are to move counter-clock-wise when the music starts or when the whistle blows, etc. When the music stops, participants must sit down on the closest empty chair available. There's one catch, the game is played in the dark. When the music starts have someone turn the lights out. When the music stops the lights go back on. Be prepared for a lot of scrambling, and running for chairs. The person left standing is out. Be sure to take one chair out after each round, and move the remaining chairs closer together as the group gets smaller. Kids have a lot of fun playing this one and usually the girls are more aggressive than the boys. (Contributed by Frank Zolvinski, La Porte, Indiana)

BLIND SARDINES

Here's a good game that is not only fun, but encourages community building within the group. There are no "winners" or "losers" in the traditional sense. All you need is a large room and blindfolds for everyone.

One person is appointed (or volunteers) to be the "sardine." The sardine does not wear a blindfold. All the other persons wear blindfolds and their objective is to come into contact with the sardine. When a person wearing a blindfold touches or runs into another person, he asks that person if he is the sardine. The sardine must say yes if touched. Once a person touches the sardine, he must hold onto the sardine for the remainder of the game, so that a chain of people is gradually formed. If a person touches anyone in the chain, it is as if he touched the sardine, and he adds himself to the chain. The sardine must not attempt to avoid being touched by anybody and is free to walk about the room. The game concludes when all are a part of the chain. (Contributed by Thomas M. Church, Bartlesville, Oklahoma)

BLIND WATER BALLOON VOLLEYBALL

This variation of volleyball combines "Blind Volleyball" with "Water Balloon Volleyball," and it is great fun when the weather is hot. Have the kids wear their swimsuits or shorts, and divide into two teams, one on each side of the volleyball net. The net, however, should be draped with blankets or some other material so that the opposing teams cannot see each other. Have on hand a good supply of water balloons. The first team "serves" the filled water balloon over the net by tossing it over. All tosses must be underhanded (as opposed to throwing them hard and fast). The receiving team must catch the water balloon without breaking it. The person who catches it then tosses it back over the net, and the same thing repeats. Any team that lets the balloon break on their side of the court, or throws the water balloon out of bounds, loses the serve or the point. It might also be a good idea to run a string or line above the net (approximately 15 feet high), and make sure the kids throw the balloon over that string. That insures that there will be no line drive tosses, or "spiking" the water balloons. The surprise element of not being able to see the water balloon until it comes over the net really adds to the excitement and fun. (Contributed by Elene Harger, Lubbock, Texas)

BOARD GAME ROTATION

Here is a better way to have an evening of board games without being "bored." Set up tables in a circle with a different 2-player board game on each table. Put chairs on two sides of the table with half the chairs facing out and half the chairs facing in towards the circle.

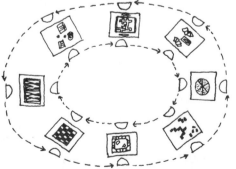

Have everyone take a seat. The games begin and continue until the whistle is blown after about 5 minutes. Both of the circles

33

then rotate to their right so that each person now moves to a different game with a different opponent. The games, however, are not reset, but the new players just take over where the last players left off. So a person might move from a winning Checkers game to a losing position in Yahtzee.

Each game is worth a set amount and that "team" (inner circle or outer circle) is given credit for the win and the games are started again. Obviously this works well as a mixer since everybody winds up playing against almost everybody else.

Other Tips: large groups may need several circles. Four person games like Rook of Monopoly can be used, but you would need to set up a rotation which is merely more complex. Use games that everyone already knows how to play or games which are simple enough to teach easily at the beginning. (Contributed by Brent Baker and John McJilton, Washington, D.C.)

BOMBS AWAY

For this game, you will need to make a partition out of cardboard or plywood (or whatever you have handy) that is about five or six feet tall. It should be about the same width, and should have a hole cut in it that is about ten inches in diameter somewhere near the top. The partition can be free-standing, or you can have two people hold it upright on each end while the game is going on.

Next, divide into teams. One person from each team lies down on the floor facing up with his feet toward the partition (under the hole). The rest of the team lines up on the other side of the partition. Each person has a water balloon (or you can use eggs). The object is for players to kneel down on the "tossing line," and to toss the water balloon (or egg) through the hole so that the person lying down on the other side can catch it before it breaks. No warning or signal can be given before tossing the water balloon. The team that has the most unbroken water balloons (or eggs) after every person has tossed (or at the end of a time limit) is the winner. It's a messy game that can be a lot of fun. (Contributed by Brenda Clowers, Bethany, Oklahoma)

BOOK VOLLEYBALL

This idea is another adaptation to the old game of volleyball. It's just like regular volleyball with two exceptions. First, everyone must use a book (any size) instead of their hands. They use the book to hit the ball. Obviously it is best to use a hardbound book. Second, a tennis ball or nerf ball is used instead of a volleyball. The rest of the usual volleyball rules apply. (Contributed by Doug Simpson, Minerva, Ohio)

BOTTLE BALL

Here's a group game which can be played indoors or out. The ideal number for this game is 5 for each side, but it can be adapted for more depending on the size of your group. Make distinguishable boundaries, approximately 60 ft. by 30 ft. The three end players must guard two bottles each. (The large plastic

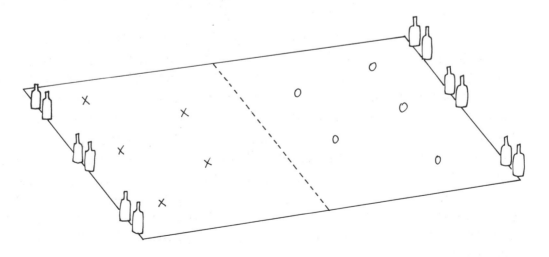

pop bottles work ideally.) These bottles should be placed about 18 inches apart. The throwers try to shoot a medium size nerf basketball (or another soft-type ball) through the opposite side, their opponents blocking the ball as best they can. Players foul when they step beyond the midway line. The scoring goes like this: 5 points for each bottle knocked down. Ten points for each shot that goes between the bottles. One point for each shot rolling over the back boundary line. Divide your group into four or six or eight different teams and have a tournament. (Contributed by J. Russell Matzke, Colorado Springs, Colorado)

CENTIPEDE RACE

Here's a great game that can be played indoors or out. All you need are some benches. Seat as many kids on each bench as possible, straddling it like a horse. When the race starts, everyone must stand up, bend over and pick up the bench, holding it between their legs. They then run like a centipede. The finish line should be 40 or 50 feet away. It's a lot of fun to watch. (Contributed by Alan Overland, Sturgeon Lake, Minnesota)

CHAIN TAG

Here is a fast-moving game that can be played both indoors or outdoors. It's a game of tag where one person begins as "it," and his job is to catch people (or tag them). When he catches someone then the two of them join hands and continue catching people as a unit. Once there is eight in the group altogether, it breaks apart and becomes two groups of four. This continues with each group of four trying to catch the remaining people. Every time they catch four more, they break off and form a new group of four. The result is several groups of four chasing the free single players who have not been caught yet. The game is played until everyone is caught. Running in groups is a lot of fun and the effect is something like "crack the whip." (Contributed by Joyce Bartlett, Liberty, New Jersey)

CHAIRBALL

This game is an exciting version of basketball that can be played on any open field or large room. Instead of using a regular basketball, use a ball that is a bit lighter, like a playground ball or a "nerf-ball." You may have any number of people on the two teams. At each end of the playing area, have someone standing on a chair holding a wastebasket, or a similar container. A jump ball starts the game, just like regular basketball. The players then try to move the ball down the field so that someone on the

team can shoot a basket. The person on the chair who is holding the basket may try to help by moving the basket if necessary to try and catch the ball when it is shot. All shots must be made beyond a ten-foot foul line. The ball may only be moved downfield by throwing it to a teammate or by kicking it. You may not run or walk with the ball. You may score baskets just like regular basketball, or you can come up with any point system that you choose. (Contributed by Julie Von Vett, Minneapolis, Minnesota)

CLUMPS TAG

Here's a great game which combines "Tag" with "Clumps." It can be played with any number of people. It should be played in a space that has boundaries, like a large room or on a basketball court. One person is "It." The leader should have either a PA system or a loud referee whistle.

The game begins with everyone milling around, including the person who is "It." It may not tag anyone yet, but as soon as the whistle is blown, he may begin to tag people who must leave the game. The referee blows the whistle a certain number of times, in quick succession. For example, if the referee blows the whistle three times, people try to get into a group of three, just like in the game "Clumps." Anyone who is in a group of three, cannot be tagged by "It." "It" should have approximately 30 seconds to try to tag as many as he can. When the whistle is blown again, everyone gets up and starts milling around again and are safe for the moment. The referee then blows the whistle again a certain number of times, and again everyone must get into the appropriate size group and lock arms in order to be safe from "It." The game continues with the referee constantly changing the number of people that are to get into groups. There will almost always be extra people running around madly without a group and its safety. If you have a PA system, or if the referee can yell loud enough, the game could be played by simply yelling out the appropriate number rather than using the whistle as described above. Each time, those people who are tagged must leave the game, and the winner or winners are those people who are left when either the time is up or there are no more people to tag. For larger groups, you might have more than one "It." It also will help if "It" has a crazy hat or shirt or something that would help everyone know who he is. (Contributed by Joe Srebro, Jerseyville, Illinois)

CROAK BALL

This is an open field game that is played just like soccer, except that you use an old volleyball and croquet mallets turned sideways. The kids must *push* the ball with the mallets (no swinging the mallets to hit the ball). Put five to ten kids on each team, mark off goals similar to soccer goals, and make up any other rules that you may find necessary. Each team should have a goalie, but the goalie doesn't have to stay near the goal unless the other team is threatening to score. (Contributed by Dick Moore, Vista, California)

CROCK BALL

This game is a lot like "Polish Baseball" (See *IDEAS Number Thirteen*), but involves the use of a two-foot high wastebasket (the crock). There are also a few rule changes. The wastebasket is turned upside down and acts as home plate. First base is about 30 to 40 feet away from home plate. There are no other bases.

The playing field is 360 degrees around home base. In other words, there are no foul areas. A pitcher's mound is placed about 20 feet from home. The batter may use any type of a bat and must hit the ball (which is a large playground ball or volleyball, slightly deflated) so that it does not knock over the crock. After hitting the ball, he or she must run to first base and back and must touch home base, thus scoring a run. The opposing players chase down the ball and must throw it to the pitcher, who must knock over the crock, thus making an out. The batter may choose to run from home to first several times if he/she hits a long ball. That way a person could score several runs all by themselves.

The pitcher should change every inning, so that one person does not dominate the game. The pitch must be lobbed up over the crock in an under hand manner, and the batter may wait for a pitch that is in the strike zone. If the pitcher knocks over the crock, then a run is scored for the team that is at bat. An umpire to call balls and strikes is optional. Once the batter swings, that's it. Even if he misses the ball, it's a fair ball, and the ball is in play. The only way to get the batter out is to knock over the crock, even on fly balls that are caught in the air. You could call caught fly balls an out if you want. Sometimes it is a good idea if you have some hard hitters who consistently hit the ball for distance. It forces them to get it on the ground.
(Contributed by George Wood, Colorado Springs, Colorado)

CRUMBLING PYRAMIDS

Divide your teens into groups of six. A team receives points when they are first to complete the instructions given. They must form a complete pyramid and then do the instructions. Following each time they must dismantle and begin when you say "Go!" Scale your points according to the number in the pyramid involved in the action if you make up more instructions.

1. Form a pyramid and say "The Pledge of Allegiance" in unison. (60 points)
2. The "Bottom Person" in the middle must take off his shoes. (20 points)
3. The "two people on the second level" must turn completely around. (40 points)
4. The "person on the top" must comb through both sides of "the person on the bottom left's" hair. (20 points)
5. The "person on the second level on the left" must turn around. (20 points)
6. The "middle person on the bottom" must turn around. (20 points)
7. The whole team turns around in a circle (only the bottom 3 have to move). (60 points)
(Contributed by Andy Strachan, Keithville, Louisiana)

DEAR HUNT

This is a good outdoor game which works best with larger groups at a camp or anywhere there is a lot of room to run around and hide. There are two teams, the boys and the girls. Teams do not have to be even. If the guys outnumber the girls two to one, for example, then you can make the scoring work out so that the girls get more points for each score than the boys do.

The object of the game is to accumulate as many points as possible by "kissing" a member of the opposite team and then having your "kiss" validated at one of the three "Cupid Stations" in your team's territory.

Both teams start off in their own territory (so designated beforehand), which is loosely half the field of play. Once the signal is given to begin, the players begin chasing name members of the opposite team, trying to "kiss" them, which is done by yanking a name tag (which is a 3x5 card) hanging from their wrist on a piece of string and a rubber band.

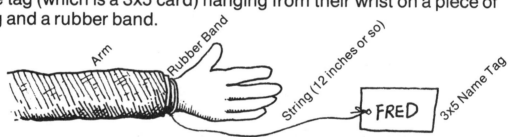

Whoever yanks off the tag first has "kissed" the opposing player and that player must then "faint" (fall down) and cease all activity at that moment. After a few moments, the faint player must rise and go to the "Hospital for the Love Sick" and stay there until he or she is able to gain a "new lease on life." This could be for five minutes or so. A new name tag is made by the resident doctor, and the player is allowed to re-enter the game.

Meanwhile, the player who makes the successful "kiss" continues to "play the field," looking for other prospects and trying to keep from getting kissed by an enemy team member. Once a player has made one or more successful kisses, he or she must get his or her captured tags validated if they are to count toward the team's overall points. This is done by getting to one of three Cupid Stations in their team's area. A Cupid Station is a clearly marked off area where official adult "cupids" wait to validate tags. Once a player is inside a cupid station they are safe from attack—but they can only enter if they have tags that need to be validated. Entering without unvalidated tags causes you to take a "lover's leap" out of the game completely. Tags can only be validated once. Tags are validated by a Cupid signing them on the back and totalling up the combined points and registering these on an official score sheet. If a player fails to make it back to a Cupid Station before getting "kissed", they loose the value of any unvalidated tags they hold.

Certain things are not allowed on the "field of play"—namely holding of any sort, tripping, kicking, or shoving (in general, anything which would not be allowed on a basketball court). Name tags cannot be concealed or held.

There will be adult "chaperones" watching the play. They have automatic authority to call a halt to any illegal activity and to penalize the offending team 50 points for each violation. Failure to heed a warning or prohibition by a chaperone will result in a 300 point penalty and removal from the game of the offending party.

Each validated "Kiss" is worth 20 points. Once the signal is given for the game to end, all persons holding or saving unvalidated tags loose their point value. All Cupids will hand in their score sheets. All Chaperones their penalty cards. From these the total score minus any penalties will be determined. The team with the most points after penalties wins! (Contributed by Phil Kennemer, Elgin, Texas)

DONKEY BASKETBALL

Remember those wooden riding horses made out of broomsticks? You can still buy them, or you can make them and use them to play Donkey Basketball. You play it just like you would regular basketball, except that you must "ride" your horse around the court while you play. It's not only fun to do, but it makes for a great spectator sport. (Contributed by Donna McElrath, Upper Marlboro, Maryland)

ELIMINATION VOLLEYBALL

Here is another version of volleyball that is a lot of fun. Divide your group into two teams, and play a regular volleyball game except that whoever makes a mistake or misses the ball goes out of the game. The teams keep getting smaller and smaller, and the team that manages to survive the longest is the winner. (Contributed by Judy Groen, Renville, Minnesota)

EQUAL RIGHTS PING-PONG

Divide your group into teams of guys and girls. The size of the teams depends on the number in your group. In this game, the rules are the same as regular ping-pong except for one minor change. On the side of the table that the girls are defending, a large bowl (12 inch diameter minimum) is placed to one side. The object of the game is to eliminate your opponent from the game by scoring a point. The only way that the guys can score a point is by hitting the bowl that is placed on the table. The ball cannot be hit until it hits the table or the bowl. This prevents blocking the bowl. This game works best with 10-15 on a team. Team members alternate on each point, so long as they remain in the game. The team that survives the longest is the winner. (Contributed by David J. Beguin, Rocky Hill, Connecticut)

FARKLE

The object of this game is to score as much *over* 5000 points as possible by throwing six dice. Points are scored in this manner:

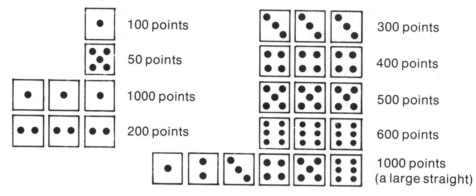

Any three of a kind or large straight must be rolled in one roll, not accumulated in more than one roll. The player starts by rolling all six dice. After rolling, he has the option of ending his turn and adding the score of his dice to his accumulated game score; or putting aside one or more of his dice that score, and rolling the remaining dice. He may continue to do this until he either decides to stop, or scores nothing on the dice he rolls. Any time a player rolls dice and scores nothing on the dice he rolled, he immediately loses his turn and all points accumulated on that turn. This is known as a "Farkle". Whenever he ends up with all six dice scoring points, whether in one turn or in several, he has "turned them over," in which case he may pick all six dice up and roll them again, adding to his accumulated score on that turn, until he chooses to stop or farkles. If he farkles, he loses *all* points accumulated on that turn, including those before he turned them over. Thus, a player's score is not added until he chooses to stop. Once a player sets aside a scoring die or dice, he may not roll them again until he turns over all six dice. A player's *first* score, to get into the game, must be at least 500 on that turn. If he doesn't score 500 points before he farkles, he must try again on his next turn. Play goes around the circle until a player accumulates 5000 or more points. At this point, his game is over, and everyone else has only one more turn—a last chance to pass him. Whoever ends then with the highest score wins.

Farkle is a good party game because any number can play, it's simple, and it promotes conversation. It also tests the balance between a player's greed and good judgment! (Contributed by David Oakes, Albuquerque, New Mexico)

FEELINGS

Feelings is a great game to get a group working together or into a line to eat lunch, go to recess, or go home. Sometimes the game resembles a mass of fumbling ducks.

A group of 20 members or less is ideal. A larger group may cause problems not to mention the stress and heartache. The group closes it's eyes and attempts to form a line in order of height. The tallest on one end and the shortest on the other. The trick is no one can speak. It seems that everyone who participates has lost their voice.

When the group has decided they have completed their task, they regain their sight. However, they never regain their voices. To get their voices back, they have to rearrange the line in order of birthdates. The person who was born closest to January is at one end. The person whose birthday is closest to December 31st is at the other end. (Contributed by Fred Bayley, Morganton, North Carolina)

FINGERS UP PLAYOFFS

Have the entire group pair off and play the game "Fingers Up." Two people face one another with their hands behind their backs. On the count of three, they bring out both hands in front of

them with a certain number of fingers on each hand held up. They should hold their hands and fingers up right in front of their face so the other person can see them. A closed fist means a zero on that hand. The first person to give the total number of fingers up on all four hands wins the game. Each pair should go for the best two out of three. The game requires quick thinking and is a lot of fun to play.

After everyone has done this, all of the losers sit down on the floor, and all the winners pair off again and play the game amongst themselves, with the losers each time sitting down and the winners pairing off. It should wind down to a championship match with two people. Give the winner a pair of gloves, some hand cream, or some crazy prize that has to do with fingers. (Contributed by Glenn G. Davis, Winston-Salem, North Carolina)

FLIP FLOP HOCKEY

Here's a new way to put a pool table to use if you have one. You only need one billiard ball, and six kids, each armed with one "Flip-Flop" (or "Thong" or "Zorie" or whatever you call those Japanese-style sandals). The heavier Flip-Flops are best. Each player guards one pocket on the pool table with his Flip-Flop. The game begins when the server serves the ball hitting it with the Flip-Flop. The ball must hit one cushion before any other player touches it. If a player touches it first, the server gets a free shot at that player's pocket. Once the ball is served, any player can hit the ball with his Flip-Flop until it goes into someone's pocket. If you successfully hit the ball into someone else's pocket, you score a point. If someone hits the ball into your own pocket, you lose a point. If there are more than six kids who want to play, have them line up on one end of the table. Then, whenever someone scores a point, rather than the defending player losing a point, he or she is simply knocked out of the game, goes to the end of the line and the next player takes his place.

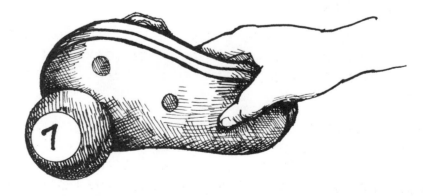

44

After each point is scored, all players rotate around the table so that everyone has a chance to play all the positions. The game can be played as described above (with each person playing individually), or you can create team competition, with two teams each guarding three pockets. Or you can create a completely new game by changing the rules any way you want. (Contributed by John Davenport, Hemet, California)

GOLFENNIS

This is simply a type of golf game using tennis balls instead of regular golf balls. Provide the kids with plenty of tennis balls, golf clubs (7 irons work best) and an open space (like a golf course, or a football field). You can't play regular golf (tennis balls are too big to go in the little holes, for one thing), but you can play lots of other games this way. For example, you could have a relay race in which teams line up, with half the team on one end of the field, and the other half of the team on the other end of the field, about 100 yards away (see diagram). The first person in line must hit the ball to the first person on the other half of his team as quickly as possible, and then that person returns it back to the original end of the field, and so on until all the players have hit. The first team to complete this task wins. It's a lot of fun, and when you are in a hurry, a tennis ball hit by a golf club can go anywhere. (Contributed by Doug Larson, Boise, Idaho)

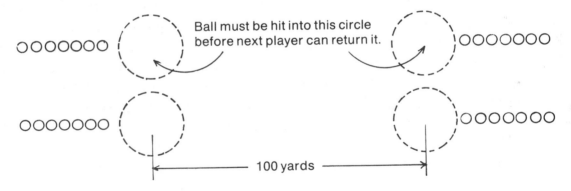

GREYHOUND RACE

Here's a fun relay-type game which requires that you set up some sort of a "racetrack." The track could be an oval, or it can be an obstacle course, or you could use the hallways of your church.

The first person on each team gets down on their hands and knees and must run on all fours, like a dog. They are given a dog's "Teething Bone" or a reasonable facsimile, which they must hold in their teeth while they run their portion of the race.

45

When they are finished with a lap around the track, or the first leg of the race, they must pass the bone to the next team member without using their hands. Give the winning team cans of dogfood. (Contributed by Renee LiaBraaten, Moorhead, Minnesota)

HILLSIDE HAVOC

If you have a nice open hillside, you might be able to add some new excitement to some of your favorite games such as baseball, volleyball, soccer, capture the flag, and so on. You can play either up, down, or across the hill, depnding on the game. If you're trying to even up two unequal sides in competition, use the hillside to give one side the advantage. This works especially well when you have competition with boys against the girls. If the teams are not unequal, play games in halves, switching sides in the middle of the game. It really adds a new dimension to game-playing. (Contributed by Alan Overland, Sturgeon Lake, Minnesota)

HUMAN FOOTBALL

Here's a wild game that can be played on any rectangular-shaped playing field, outdoors or indoors. A normal football field works fine. There are two teams, the offense and the defense. There can be any number on each team, boys or girls.

When a team is on offense, they begin play at the 20-yard line. They get four downs to move the ball down the field and to score a touchdown. There are no additional first downs. The way yardage is made is for the team on offense to hike the ball to its quarterback, who is then picked up and carried by the rest of the team down the field. The entire team must be joined together, either carrying the quarterback or by holding on to the team members who are carrying the quarterback.

The defensive team begins each play lined up on the goal line which they are defending. As soon as the offensive team hikes the ball, the defensive team locks arms and moves down the field toward the offensive team, now on the move towards them. When the defensive team reaches the offensive team, the two end members of the defense try to dislodge one of the offensive players from the rest of their team. As soon as this is accomplished, the down is over. The ball is then put into play from that point. The defensive team returns to the goal line on each play, and the offensive team repeats the same procedure. If no touchdown is scored in four tries, the defense becomes the offense and gets the ball at the 20 yard line going the other direction. All teams must walk while the ball is in play. If the defense breaks its chain, they must reunite before proceeding down the field. If the offensive chain breaks, the down is automatically over. Score the game any way you wish. (Contributed by Greg Tyree, Yakima, Washington)

HUMAN PIT

Here is a great game for camp or large youth groups, that is based on the popular game of "Pit," produced by Parker Brothers. It is a card game, but instead of using cards, you use people as cards.

Here's how to play. First of all, decide on the commodity to be traded (like animals, sports teams, schools, colors, and so on). Then determine the number of teams you wish to have. For each team, there must be nine cards of one suit. For example, if you have three teams, and you are using animals, there must be nine dogs, nine cats, and nine pigs, or whatever animals you decide to use. You will want at least two people on each team (the teams are the people who are not cards). The more teams you have, the more chaotic and fun the game is. For each suit chosen, make nine slips of paper which will identify the suit. For example, if your suits are colors, and one of the colors is red, make nine red slips of paper. Bring enough pins to pin these pieces of paper onto the people who will be cards.

Now you must choose people to be cards. If you have seven teams, you will need to choose 63 cards (nine times seven). Have everyone stand in a large circle and count off the number of cards needed. Instruct the "cards" to go to the middle of the circle where several assistants help with pinning the pieces of paper identifying their suit on the *inside* of their sweaters, cuffs or whatever, so that their suit is not outwardly visible. While the cards are being prepared in the middle, number off the remaining teams. Space each team evenly around the outside of the circle. Instruct each team to then choose one master trader to be responsible for trading cards for their team in the middle of the circle (the Pit).

Deal the cards to the teams by having nine "cards" randomly go to each team. From this point on, cards must move on their hands and knees. Be sure each team has nine cards and has a little time to identify the suit of the cards.

Now you are ready to start the trading. Announce that all trading is to be done in the "Pit" and only by the master trader on each team. To trade, a team must choose one to four cards of the same suit. The master trader then leads the cards to be traded (on their hands and knees) to the middle where he calls out "Trade one! One! One!" or "Two! Two! Two!" or "Three! Three! Three!" or "Four! Four! Four!" depending on the number of cards being traded. If the trader of one team wishes to trade cards with another team, he must call out "One! One! One!" etc., and trade an equal number of cards with that team. When cards have been exchanged, each master trader must bring his new cards (on their hands and knees) back to his team before looking to see what suit the cards are that he has received. Then the team decides what cards they wish to trade next, and so on. Trading continues until one team gets nine cards of the same suit and wins the game.

After explaining all this, let them begin. It is a fast moving game and is hilarious to watch. There is usually absolute mayhem in the middle of the "Pit." Following the game you may want to discuss how the cards felt when teams wanted to keep them or wanted to get rid of them. Play as many rounds as you have time for. This idea could also be transferred to many other card games, by simply substituting people for playing cards. (Contributed by Chris Keidel, Flourtown, Pennsylvania)

KICK THE TIRE

This is simply a game of "kickball," using an old innertube instead of a rubber ball. Fill the tube quite full, and the pitcher rolls the tube up to home plate, where the kicker gives it a swift kick. It may fly, roll, flop, bounce, no one really knows. The kicker can be put out by a fly that is caught, or if he is hit with the tube enroute to the base. Or you can have force outs, just like regular baseball. Whatever rules you decide to use, this variation of an old game is lots of fun. (Contributed by Glenn Hermann, Richfield, Minnesota)

LEMON SHOOT OUT

Here's a great game for hot, summer days. Recycle store-bought plastic lemons which contain lemon and/or lime juice. Fill the plastic lemons which are capable of squirting with water. Line up participants of the game into two lines, each team facing each other approximately ten feet apart, equipping each person with a lit candle and a water-filled plastic lemon. Have each person put the lit candle in front of his/her face. On the call of "go" all participants will try to extinguish the candle flames of the opposing team. First team to extinguish the other team's candles wins. This game can also be played with squirt guns. It is obviously an outdoor game. (Contributed by Grant Lee, Honolulu, Hawaii)

LET IT BLOW

Divide your group into teams and give each person a deflated balloon. On a signal, the first person on each team blows up his/her balloon and lets it go. The balloon will sail through the air.

That person must then go to where it lands, stop and blow it up again and let it go. The object is to get the balloon across a goal line some distance away. When he does, he can run back and tag the next player on the team, and then that person must do the same thing. This game is really wild, since it is almost impossible to predict where the balloons will land each time. It is especially fun and interesting when played outside, because the slightest breeze blows the balloon in a different direction. The goal line should be about 15 feet away. (Contributed by Judy Groen, Renville, Minnesota)

MAD MAD MATTRESS

For this game divide your group into several teams. Each team needs a mattress. If the mattresses are small, then give each team two mattresses that are placed side by side; or if the mattress is small, then tailor the events to fit the size of the mattress. The team stands around the outside of the mattress.

The leader then gives an instruction, and each team must perform that task on the mattress. The first team to correctly complete the task receives points for that round. Each task must be completed entirely on the mattress. Some sample tasks:

1. Build a six (or 10) person pyramid.
2. Get 12 people sitting in a circle with their feet together in the middle.
3. Get 4 people to stand on their heads in each of the four corners of the mattress.
4. Get the whole team on the mattress. (Works good if you have large groups.)
5. Get 4 girls up on 4 guys' shoulders.
6. Get 15 people laying flat on their stomachs, side by side.

You can make up more tasks of your own. It might be a good idea to have a referree at each mattress to determine when the task has been completed successfully. (Contributed by Judy Groen, Renville, Minnesota)

MARBLE SUCKING RELAY

For this game divide your group into several teams. Give each person a plastic straw and a paper cup. The first person on each team gets a marble in his cup. The object is to suck the marble up with the straw and drop it into the next person's cup. If the marble drops on the floor, the team must start over at the beginning. The first team to get the marble to the last person on the team wins. (Contributed by Judy Groen, Renville, Minnesota)

MARSHMALLOW SURPRISE

At first this game seems mild and old fashioned. You hang a line and on the line you tie marshmallows to strings about 18 inches long. You ask for volunteers to try to eat the marshmallows off the strings without using their hands. When they get up there you ask for volunteers to coach each participant. The coaches must tie blindfolds on each person and back them up about three or four feet from the line. After each person is blindfolded you go over the rules real slow so that another person has enough time to come along with a can of Hershey's chocolate syrup and dip each marshmallow. At a signal the coach verbally directs their person to their marshmallow and tells him or her how close they're getting, etc. The coach must make sure that the participants don't use their hands. Amazingly enough, very few realize that they are making a mess all over their face. The spectators are really getting a good laugh.

Another way to do this is to remove the marshmallows altogether. It's a riot to watch kids hunting with their mouths for something that is not there. Coaches should be clued in. (Contributed by Brenda Clowers, Bethany, Oklahoma)

ODDBALL MIXER

Here's a good mixer or game for almost any size group. Before the game begins, have ten guys and ten girls prepare themselves to fit the descriptions on the lists below. This should be kept somewhat secret until the game begins. Then, give each person a list like those below. You can use one list for everyone, or you can prepare two separate ones, one for the guys and one for the girls. The idea is simply to try and be the first person to find the people who fit the descriptions and to write in their names. You can make up your own descriptions. The ones given are only suggestions.

For the girls: Find the boy who. . .

1. Has a red comb in his back pocket_____
2. Has a rubber band around his sock_____
3. Has his wrist watch on upside down_____
4. Has his shoes on the wrong feet_____
5. Has a thumb tack in the heel of his right shoe_____

6. Has a bobby pin in his hair_____
7. Has a band-aid on his neck_____
8. Has his shoe laced from the top down_____
9. Has only one sock on_____
10. Has his belt on upside down_____

For the guys: Find the girl who. . .

1. Has one earring on_____
2. Has a rubber band around her wrist_____
3. Has on mis-matched earrings_____
4. Has a penny in her shoe_____
5. Has lipstick on her ear_____
6. Has a paper clip on her collar_____
7. Has nail polish on one fingernail_____
8. Has on one false eyelash_____
9. Is chewing bubble gum_____
10. Has on one nylon stocking_____

(Contributed by Mrs. F. S. Richardett, Howell, New Jersey)

PING PONG BASEBALL

Here's a good baseball game that you can play indoors. All you need are ping pong balls, and a ping pong paddle for the bat. It requires a lot of room, and is very fast-moving and exciting to play. If the ball hits the roof on a fly, it is playable, but the walls are foul territory. It's a great game for rainy days or anytime you want to have something indoors. All the usual rules of baseball apply. (Contributed by Keith Robinson, Minneapolis, Minnesota)

PING PONG BALL IN THE CUP

Here's a game that is not only fun to play but is fun to watch. The only props you need are an ordinary ping pong ball and a plastic drinking cup. With boundaries (approximately 20 feet between pitcher and catcher), have one person throw the ball with a teammate catching the ball in the cup. A catcher cannot use his hands, and must catch the ball before it quits bouncing. The patience required to catch this ball in the cup makes this game very entertaining in a large room that has a cement or tile floor, providing plenty of bounce. You could award points for the number of bounces before the ball is caught. (Contributed by Glenn G. Davis, Winston-Salem, North Carolina)

PING PONG BLOW DRY

Here's a crazy relay game involving use of blow dryers (the kind you use to dry your hair), one large wash tub or some other kind of container, and some ping pong balls. This game is best for two or three teams. Each team has a ping pong ball in the tub, with a different color ping pong ball for each team. The tub containing the ball is placed 20 feet or so away from the teams. On go, the first person at the head of the line runs to the tub, picks up the dryer and attempts to get their team ball out of the tub using the blow dryer to blow it out. When this is accomplished, that person puts the ball back in the tub and goes to the end of the line, and the second person repeats the procedure. When two or three people are trying to blow their ping pong ball out of the tub at the same time, it's fun to watch what happens. You might want to try out the blow dryers and wash tubs, etc. before you play this game just to be sure that it works. Do not put water in the wash tub. (Contributed by Steve Hopper, Stanwood, Washington)

PONY EXPRESS

This is an outdoor game that requires a paved area, bicycles, step-ladders, and the use of water. It's a great game for a warm, sunny day.

Divide into teams of any number, depending on how many bicycles and ladders you have. Form a circular track, with ladders lining the inside of the track (see diagram). Each ladder has a bucket of water on it and a paper cup.

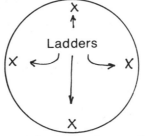

Bike riders are equipped with containers tied to their heads. You can take an old straw hat, turn it upside down and cut slits through it with a scarf through the slits. Tie the scarf under the chin. Line the inside of the hat with plastic and place a plastic bowl in the hat. The straw-hat shaped containers that potted plants come in are perfect. The illustration below might help!

Bowl inside upside-down hat

Ribbon tied under chin

Riders then get on the bicycles (with their hats on) and ride around in the circle as close to the ladders as possible. Teammates are stationed on the ladders, and they try to toss water in the hats of the riders as they ride by. After each lap, the riders dump off their water into a container, and continue until the time limit is up (five minutes is usually sufficient, but it could be longer). Each team goes separately and the team that collects the most water within the time limit is the winner.

If the above procedure seems too complicated, try playing this game with your own set-up. For example, the bike riders could carry water containers on baskets held onto the handlebars, or they could be pulling wagons with buckets in them, or whatever. Use your imagination. You could substitute tricycles for bicycles, or just have the kids run around the circle instead of using bikes. The possibilities are endless. (Contributed by Brenda Clowers, Bethany, Oklahoma)

POT SHOT

Divide the group into two even relay teams. Each team lines up sitting on the floor behind each other with their backs turned toward "the pot" (a toilet seat) at the far end of the two rows. Two "nerf" balls are started at each row. The first person, of each row, takes the ball by clamping the ball between his or her wrists. Still sitting, he turns around to the next person and passes it from his wrists to their wrists, and so on down the line. No hands are used until the ball reaches the last person, then he or she shoots the ball through the pot, with retrievers chasing and throwing back the missed "pot shots." The shooter stays seated and shooting until the shot is made. Then he moves with the ball to the back of the line, the row shifts, and the sequence is repeated until the last person has shot successfully. Recommended shooting distance is about 5 feet. Players should be spaced about 3 feet apart. (Contributed by Mark Simpson, Everett, Washington)

SEVEN-LEGGED RACE

Divide the kids into two teams. Have everyone pair off with someone

of their own team and get into "crab" position. With fabric scraps (they don't hurt) tie a right arm to the left arm of each pair of kids. Have them race relay style to a set place and back again, one pair at a time. The first team to finish wins. (Contributed by Jim Walton, Fitchburg, Massachusetts)

SIAMESE SOFTBALL

This is a perfect game for a group too large to play a regular softball game. Teams are evenly divided and team members are paired by hooking their arms together. At no time while playing are they allowed to unhook their arms or use their hooked arms. They may use their free arms and hands. A rubber ball or volleyball is used instead of a softball because it can be caught with the pair's free arms and hands. Only one person needs to throw the ball.

When at bat, pairs are to grasp the bat with their free hands together. After the ball is hit, the pair must run the bases with arms hooked together. Other than these exceptions everything else is played with regular softball rules. (Contributed by Michael Allen, Occidental, California)

SOCKEY

Here's a great outdoor game that features elements from two other popular games—Soccer and Hockey. In order to play, you will need a large playing field, two hockey sticks, a soccer ball, and a couple of medium sized cardboard boxes for hockey goals. The playing field is laid out like the diagram below, with two marked circles approximately 10 ft. in diameter at opposite ends of the playing field. The cardboard boxes (goals) should be another 10 to 15 feet away from the circles.

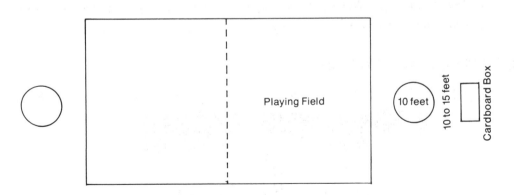

Divide the kids into two teams. Each team places one player with the hockey stick in the circle. He cannot leave the circle and no other player may enter the circle. The team must kick the ball to the circle containing their player. Hands cannot be used at any time. Once the ball is kicked into the circle, the player in the circle grabs the ball, places it and tries to hit it into the cardboard box with the hockey stick. If he succeeds he scores points for his team. If he misses, then it's a point for the opposing team. After each point is attempted, the ball is returned to midfield and play resumes. It is usually a good idea to rotate the player within the circle so everyone has a chance to score, and so that no one player can dominate the game. (Contributed by Doug Newhouse, Florence, Kentucky)

SODA POP RELAY

This is a relay game with a fun ending. All you do is have teams line up in normal relay fashion. The first person in each line gets a can opener. Out in front of the team some distance away is a bottle of soda pop—the type that needs to be opened with a can opener. Each person on the team has to run around the bottle of pop, and return to the team passing the can opener to the next player. When the can opener gets back to the first person again, that person runs out to the bottle of pop, opens it, and drinks it. The first to do so is the winner.

To make this game more exciting, before the race, and without anyone knowing, shake the bottles of pop profusely. It also helps if you store them in a hot place before the race. (Contributed by D. C. Seville, Glendale, Arizona)

SOUND SWEEPSTAKES

Here's a simple game which is always a lot of fun. All you need is a tape recorder. Ahead of time go out and record the sounds of 20 various things, such as a light switch, car starting, the spraying of a deodorant can, and so forth. Let your mind wander and try to come up with all kinds of sounds that most people would be familiar with. Then, simply play back the sounds at your meeting. Each person must try to guess the sound and write their answer on a piece of paper. You can play by teams, by having the groups try to agree on the sound and come up with the list. Play the sounds back one at a time, and give one minute after the sound to write down their answer. At the conclusion, play back all of the sounds and review the answers. Award points for each correct guess. This game can be just as interesting as you want to make it. Be creative. (Contributed by Mike Shields, St. Paul, Minnesota)

SPEND THAT DOLLAR

Here's a game that needs to be played in a shopping area or shopping mall that has at least 10 stores in it. Divide the group into teams of 2 to 4 each. Give each team a one dollar bill. Teams are then instructed to spend that dollar on exactly ten items in exactly ten or more stores. They must return to a predetermined place with each item and a receipt for each item. There cannot be any repeats of items.

The time limit is one hour. The winner is determined by who finishes first or who has the most change leftover. The best place for them to return is to the ice cream stand in the mall, if there is one available. That way you can have a refreshment with the winning group getting their ice cream for free.

If inflation makes 10 items absolutely impossible, you could do it with larger amounts, but it is possible to buy things like this for a dime: slices of meat, cheese, bubblegum, combs, a cricket in a pet store, pencils, a cup of water in a restaurant, etc. It does take a little creativity. (Contributed by Christopher Buck, Lebanon, Oregon)

STAR WARS

Here's a game that can generate some excitement simply because of its name. The idea is to cut out dozens (or hundreds) or little cardboard stars about three or four inches wide, and play games with them. One game is to have teams line up behind a foul line and try to toss the stars into a bucket, or onto a chair, or something along those lines. Because of the shape of the stars, they don't always go exactly where they are tossed and it can be a lot of fun. Make up your own rules.

Another game would be to pattern your "Star Wars" game after the game of "Snowfight" (found in an earlier volume of *IDEAS*). Draw a line down the middle of the room, put one team on each side of the line, and give each team an equal number of cardboard stars to begin with. On "go," the object is to throw all your stars onto the opponents "space." At the end of the time limit, the team (or empire) that has the fewest stars on their side of the line is the winner. (Contributed by Jon Hantsbarger, Carthage, Missouri)

SUCK EM UP

Divide the group into three or more teams with equal amounts on each team. Line each team up behind a starting line. Place a paper bucket (like one of those fried chicken buckets or paper paint buckets) about 25-30 feet from the starting line. About two inches from the bottom of the bucket cut a round hole big enough for a ping-pong ball to pass through. Place a ping-pong ball in the bucket. Position a person at the bucket with a length of plastic plumbing pipe (one inch pipe works best, about 10 inches long).

Back at the starting line place a dish pan full of water in front of each team. Give each team member a straw. At the signal each team member must suck up some water in his straw and hold it in his mouth while he runs to the bucket and puts the water in the bucket. This goes on until the person at the bucket can take the plumbing pipe and blow the ping-pong ball out the hole in the side of the bucket. He then sucks the ball up on the end of the pipe and runs with it to the dish pan at the starting line and drops it in. The first team that gets the ball in their dishpan wins. (Contributed by Brenda Clowers, Bethany, Oklahoma)

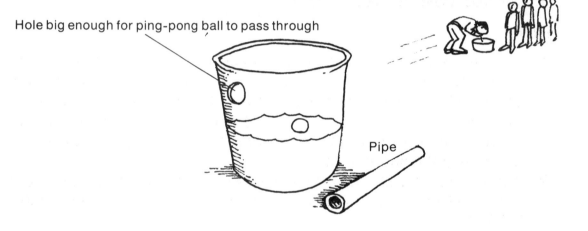

Hole big enough for ping-pong ball to pass through

Pipe

SUPERMAN VOLLEYBALL

Here's yet another way to add a new twist to the old game of volleyball. Simply play by all the normal rules, but inflate the ball with helium. It won't float away, but watch how high it goes. Everyone will feel like superman. You may need to increase the size of your volleyball court in order to accommodate the higher flight of the ball. (Contributed by Doug Newhouse, Florence, Kentucky)

TEAM CROSSWORD

Here's a good indoor game which requires some quick thinking. Get a book of crossword puzzles and select one that would be about the right difficulty for your group. Reproduce the crossword puzzle on a large piece of butcher paper, or project it on the wall with an overhead projector. Divide your group into two or more teams. When you read the "clue" the first team to shout out the right answer gets a point for every blank letter space filled.

The team with the correct answer then gets to select which clue is read next, and so forth. It's usually a good idea to have one person read the "clues," and have another person fill in the correct responses and keep score. If one team gets too far ahead, give triple point value on the last few words and give the teams that are behind a chance to catch up. (Contributed by Dan H. Prout, Ventura, California)

TUBECIDE

This game is most suitably played on a field covered with a glaze of snow. It can, however, be played on any kind of field.

Two equal teams of any size, a field of any size with no boundaries and two large, well-inflated inner tubes are the only requirements for the game. Each team must be given a goal, however. Two markers 15 feet apart will suffice for a goal.

Rules:

1. Two tubes are placed on top of each other in the center of the field. The two teams form a friendly scrum (arms over each other's shoulders in a circle). The entire group yells the word SCRUM three times. On the third SCRUM each team attempts to move their tube towards their goal. Teams are on offense and defense at the same time.
2. When a team gets their tube through their goal, they receive a point. When a goal is scored, play stops for another center SCRUM.
3. The tubes can't be touched with the hands, but it can be forwarded by any other means.
4. Hooking (putting a lag or arm through the tube and holding it) is not allowed.
5. Checking is allowed, but using hands to push or grab is not allowed.

Keep a patch kit and air pump handy. To handicap a group, give them a larger tube. Small tubes are much faster. Feel free to modify the rules as needed to keep the game safe and exciting. (Contributed by Orval Gingerich, Colorado Springs, Colorado)

TURKEY SHOOT

This is a fun little game that you can play next time you take your youth group to an amusement park or to the zoo or to any other place where they divide up into small groups and head out on their own. Give each group about ten "chips" or "tokens" (anything will do) to start with. Then, whenever one group spots another in the park, they yell "Freeze, you Turkey!" at the other group. The spotted group must then surrender one chip to the team that spotted them. At the end of the day, the group that comes back with the most chips wins a prize, or gets the best seats on the bus home, or whatever. It's a lot of fun, and it keeps the kids looking out for each other all day. (Contributed by Rob Moritz, Kansas City, Missouri)

TURTLE BASKETBALL

This idea adds a twist to the game of basketball. Instead of running up and down the court, everyone walks. Everyone, however, can walk as fast as they can. If the offense is caught running, the ball goes over to the other team. If the defense is caught, the offensive team member wins the ball and shoots two free throws. Each person caught running is assessed a foul. Also, everyone must keep their feet on the floor when rebounding. If someone is caught jumping, the ball goes to the other team. No foul is given here. This is really hilarious to watch. Except for the above, regular rules for scoring in basketball are used. (Contributed by Doug Simpson, Minerva, Ohio)

VALENTINE CANDY CHARADES

Here's a good little game for your next Valentine's Banquet. Get some of those candy "conversation" hearts that have two to three word sayings on them: "I love you," "Slick Chick," "Turtle Dove," etc. One person from the group picks out one of the candies from a bowl, and using the regular rules for charades tries to pantomime the message. The person who correctly guesses the saying gets to eat that piece of candy. You could use teams, just like regular charades or you could do it like the game "Password" with couples who try to communicate to their partners. It is really hilarious to watch the participants try to do phrases like "Lover Boy," "Kiss Me," and all the other crazy sayings that they put on those traditional candies. (Contributed by Wayne Peterson, Cedar Rapids, Michigan)

VOLLEYBALL DISCUSSION GROUPS

This game combines the fun of a volleyball game with some small group discussion. Divide into teams for a regular volleyball game. Like after every 5th point scored, have a row of players break into a small group. The leader then throws out a discussion question of the ice-breaker variety. A question such as "If you could go anywhere in the world, where would you go?" would be appropriate. Each person gets a chance to speak, and then the leader gets the team going again. Since people are supposed to rotate after every volleyball point, it means that the group will be different every time they get into small groups. This makes the game great as a mixer. (Contributed by Glen Bolger, Sparta, New Jersey)

Chapter Three

Creative Communication

AD VALUES

Give the group a selection of magazines with plenty of advertisements in them. Each person should have a magazine. Also give each person a list of values like the one below, with room beside each value to "keep score." Then have the kids go through the magazine that they have and try to match the ads with the values on their list. When they see an ad that appeals to a certain value, then they make a mark beside that value. Here is a sample list:

1. Wealth, luxury, greed
2. Security (No worries)
3. Sexual or Physical Attractiveness
4. Intelligence
5. Conformity (Join the Crowd)
6. Freedom (Do what you want—no responsibility)
7. Justice, Human Rights (Concern for others)
8. Power, Strength
9. Responsibility
10. Ego, Pride
11. Status (Being Looked Up To)
12. Escapism
13. Humility, Self-sacrifice
14. Self-control
15. Ease, Comfort

After everyone has finished, discuss the results. What conclusions can you come to about the kind of values that most advertisements present or appeal to? Do they bring out the best or the worst in people? Do very many ads appeal to "Christian" values? This exercise can really sensitize young people to be more aware of the ads that they are exposed to. (Contributed by Tim Spilker, Lakeside, California)

AMERICAN BANDSTAND

For an effective program on the good and bad of rock music, have an "American Bandstand" night. Bring in a selection of rock records that are currently popular, and have the kids vote on the ones that they like best, according to certain standards. You might find it worthwhile to get the words to the songs so that your kids will be able to follow along while listening. Then play the records and have the kids judge them using judging sheets with the following criteria:

1. *Lyrics:* What is the message of the song? Does it support or contradict Christian values and the Word of God?
2. *The Artist:* What is he or she like as a person? Are they good role models for Christian young people? Do they avoid behavior that offends those who follow Christ?
3. *Overall Effect of the Song:* Does this song make you feel more positive about your faith or about life? Or more negative? Does it strengthen you as a Christian or weaken you? Or is it neutral?

Before the kids rate the songs that they listen to, you should discuss each of the three criteria so that they know what each one means. Also, you will probably want to discuss each song individually. You may want to add another category as well: *The Music.* In this category, kids decide whether or not the record would be considered "good music" or not.

After the kids have rated all the songs, take your results and come up with your own youth group "Top 10" or "Top 5." The whole experience can really help kids to have a better sensitivity to what they listen to. (Contributed by Randy Wheeler, Portales, New Mexico)

ARE YOU SERIOUS, DR. SEUSS?

No, this is not an idea for young children. This one is for the big kids — junior high, high school, college age, or even older. It incorporates the use of some of the popular Dr. Seuss tales that are available everywhere in bookstores, children's stores, department stores, and the like. (The books are published by Random House, New York.) Most people are familiar with Dr. Seuss' nonsense books, like "The Cat in the Hat," but he also has a number of excellent books and stories that deal with some rather "heavy" topics that are ideal for discussion and/or Bible study groups.

The discussion questions that follow are based upon several of these Dr. Seuss stories. "Sneetches" is a book that deals with racism, sexism, cliques, fads, and so on. "Yertle the Turtle" deals with pride, vanity, taking advantage of others, self-concept, and the like. "The Lorax" has to do with ecology and is particularly suited for opening up discussion on the nuclear power question. All of these issues are approached by Dr. Seuss in a humorous yet profound way. You will have to buy (or get from your local library) your own Dr. Seuss books, in order for you to make much sense out of the discussion questions published here.

Some of these Dr. Seuss tales are also available on 16mm film. Check your library's film-lending department.

One great way to use this material is to put on a "Dr. Seuss Retreat," which would feature the use of these books and the following discussions. It sounds so ridiculous and bizarre that most kids will look forward to it just because it's so crazy. Along with the more serious stuff can be a variety of Dr. Seuss games (just change the names of your favorite games; e.g. "Capture the Flag" could become "The Sneetch Snatch"). You might have some of the kids act out the stories while they are being read to the group, or you could have the books transferred to slides or overhead transparencies for projection. Another (more expensive) possibility is to purchase enough copies of each book for everyone, or for each study group. But regardless of how you use these learning experiences, you'll be surprised to find just how effective and interesting they are. Most young people enjoyed Dr. Seuss when they were children, but are just now getting old enough to really appreciate what he has written. Use your own creativity as you use this material with your group. Add other discussion questions or applications as you see fit.

THE SNEETCHES

1. In your school, home, community and nation, who are the Star-bellied Sneetches? Name them as individuals or groups.

2. Who are Plain-bellied Sneetches in your home, community, school, nation? Name them as individuals or groups.

3. Are you a Plain-bellied Sneetch or a Star-bellied Sneetch? Why?

4. What really made the Star-bellied Sneetches feel "superior" and Plain-bellied feel

"inferior"? How can the Plain-bellied overcome this?

5. Name some "stars" that exist in our society. Are they good or bad?

6. Who or what might be a "Sylvester McMonkey McBean" in our society?

7. What is this story really about? What is one of the points of the story?

8. What advice does this story give for handling the problems between different groups such as women and men, rich and poor, Christians and non-Christians?

9. What does the Bible say about pride? See Luke 18:9-14, I John 2:15-17, and I Peter 5:5-6.

10. What does Galatians 3:26-29 mean and how does it apply to Sneetches?

11. What happens regarding Sneetch attitude when a person is "in Christ" or motivated by the Holy Spirit? See II Corinthians 5:16-17 (also 18-21).

12. For homework, read John 15:11-17 and then find a Plain-bellied Sneetch and befriend him/her by inviting to join in on a game after this session is over.

HORTON HEARS A WHO

1. Write the main point of this story.

2. Pretend you are either a Who (or someone trying to help a Who) at school or in your neighborhood. Who are the Wickershams and Kangaroos? What do they represent?

3. Why couldn't the Wickershams and the Kangaroos just leave Horton alone?

4. Who are some Whos you know? Name one time when you were the only one able to hear them. How did you feel then?

5. Why did Horton feel an obligation to the Whos? What drove him on?

6. Suppose that you are a Who in Whoville, but your speck is really a poison ivy seed. Christ is Horton. Will Horton still go to all the efforts he did to save the seed—even though he will surely get terminal poison ivy? Why or why not? See Romans 5:6-9.

7. Since you are a Who and have been saved from disaster because of Horton, what is your obligation and behavior to other whos and specks you should see in the light of John 15:11-17?

8. What is the point Jo-Jo adds to the story? Name some Biblical figures like him—small but able to do great things.

Homework: Find a "Who" and stick with him "through thin and through thick".

THIDWICK THE BIG HEARTED MOOSE

1. If you were Thidwick at what point would you have stopped taking hitch-hikers on your horns and why?

2. Who was responsible for Thidwick's problem? What should he have done about it, if anything?

3. Try to remember the last time you were taken advantage of and didn't say anything. Write down how you felt about yourself and the other person.

4. If you were one of the other mooses (yes, I know it's wrong) on Lake Winna-Bango what would you have said to Thidwick?

5. While you are taking an exam in school, a friend wants to ride on "your horns" or be helped. What do you say or do?

6. Pretend you are Thidwick. As a Christian moose is there ever a time when you should say no to a request and if so when and how? If not, why not?

7. Is it possible to do what Matthew 25:31-40 says and not be taken advantage of in the process? If so, how?

8. Read Colossians 3:12-15 and I Corinthians 13:4-7. As a Moose of God write down three rules about helping other mooses (yes, it's still grammatically wrong) that is in accordance with these scriptures and your answer to number 6.

Homework: Take two minutes alone today and ponder what eventually happens to the creatures who try to get a free ride. Pray for them individually.

YERTLE THE TURTLE

1. Describe the type of turtle Yertle was and was becoming before he fell. Name his emotions, characteristics and attitudes up to the falling time.

2. What kind of turtle was Mack? Describe his emotions, attitudes and characteristics.

3. If Mack is turtle #1 and Yertle is turtle #10, between 1 and 10, write down what your number is.

4. What was Yertle's real problem? Are people as a whole like this? Why or why not?

5. What was Mack's real problem? Do you know people who have this same problem?

6. According to Genesis 3:1-5, what promise did the snake in the pond make to "Eve the Turtle?" Is this still our basic problem?

7. In the story of the "Prodigal Turtle" (Luke 15:11-24) what things was the son seeking before he left home? Do you consider these bad or good things?

8. When the "Prodigal Turtle" landed in the mud, what did he realize?

9. Imagine you are Yertle and are at the top of the pile and see the moon over you. But instead of trying to be higher still, you realize that the God of the turtles gave us all we have and are, and made us not kings over other turtles but brothers with them. Realizing this and that God is above all, you become converted. What do you do and say to get down off the throne? What do you say to the other turtles when you are down? After you have written your answer, read Matthew 5:21-24.

Homework: Sometime during this retreat go find a place to sit down outside and think of yourself as a little (or a lot) like Yertle and then have a conversation with the King of the Turtles.

BARTHOLOMEW AND THE OOBLECK

1. What and who was the cause of King Derwins problem?

2. What is the moral of this story?

3. Write down the last time you were dissatisfied and why? What did you do to overcome the unhappiness?

4. Pretend that Bartholomew Cubbins is your conscience and as King you want something "NEW" that drugs or alcohol might provide. Write a summary of the conversation that you and Bartholomew have.

5. What would Christians call the moment King Derwin sobbed "I'm sorry"?

6. You are King and have made a mess of things. What must you do to set it right? After you have written your answer read Matthew 13:1-3 and John 3:1-3.

7. Why does God allow us to have things that are harmful to us or others around us? After you have written your answer read 2 Corinthians 7:8-10.

8. At several points in the Bible we are told to be "content with what we have." (Hebrews 13:5 and I Timothy 6:8) We are also told "ask anything in my name and I will give it to you". Why should we ask for things if we are supposed to be content with what we have? Is there a special attitude we should have when we ask for something? What is it? See Matthew 6:7-13 and Matthew 26:39-42.

9. For homework, take some time and list 10 things on the back of this paper that you are thankful for just the way they are.

GERTRUDE McFUZZ (In the "Yertle the Turtle" book)

1. Name three bad characteristics or evil desires of Gertrude's.

2. What is the real difference in Gertrude from the very beginning of the story and its end since she still only has one plain tail feather?

3. Imagine you are Gertrude but instead of wanting tail feathers you want something that some other bird has and you do not. What is it you want and why do you want it?

4. What did Doctor Dake say to try to convince Gertrude not to seek to have a different tail? How can this apply to human Gertrudes?

5. If you were Gertrude and could have eaten between 0 and 36 pill-berries to get what you want; at what number would you stop eating and why?

6. What did Gertrude want to do immediately after she had all the feathers she wanted? Name two times when you did what Gertrude wanted to do.

7. What was Gertrude's cure and what warning might it give to us when we behave like Gertrude?

8. Write one of the 10 Commandments that could best be applied to this story? (Exodus 20:7-17)

9. Find a Bible with an Old and New Testament and read I Samuel 16:6 & 7 and then I Peter 3:1-5. What would Gertrude say if she had read this before she had eaten a pill-berry? What would she say now?

10. For homework: The next time you see someone trying to show off their tail feathers ask "have they seen Gertrude lately?" If you catch yourself behaving like Gertrude pluck your feathers out by pinching yourself on your bottom.

THE ZAX (in the "Sneetches" book)

1. What is this story really about? What is the point?

2. Who was at fault in this argument? Who won the argument?

3. If you were a Zax and you met another, how would you solve the difference if only one of you were willing to compromise? Would you negotiate, use force, persuasion, or . . .?

4. By arguing, stubbornness, and focusing exclusively on one another, what are the Zax's

failing to see going on around them? Can you relate this to your life? The Church?

5. Have you ever been in an argument where you would not give in? When? Why wouldn't you give in? How did it end?

6. After you have read Luke 6:27-36, pretend you meet a Zax coming from the other way. In the light of Luke 6, what do you do and why?

7. How does the King of all of the Zaxes want us to behave? Read John 13:1-17 before you answer.

8. Are there any times when "giving in" to the other Zax is not acceptable? If so, when?

Homework: To help humorously solve conflict, the next time you find yourself in a confronting situation or argument, as soon as you can remember to do so ask the other person, "Are you a North-going Zax or a South-going Zax?"

THE LORAX

1. Write two of the main points this story has to offer.

2. Who do you think Dr. Seuss thinks the reader is in this story and why? Does he think we are Once-lers, Lorax or the little boy?

3. Which character do you feel like you are while reading this story? Why?

4. What do truffula trees represent? What are some of America's "truffula trees?"

5. A hydroelectric plant is being built which will provide you and 100,000 others in your area with electricity. It is learned that a small endangered species of fish will be eliminated if the dam is built. There is a conflict between the neighbors who need electricity and some young conservationist who wants to protect the fish. Whose side are you on and why?

6. What does the Lorax symbolize? What was his job and who does it (or should do it) today?

7. What are some reasonable guidelines for individuals and businesses about using our natural resources?

8. The word on the Lorax's last standing place said "Unless." Unless what?

9. Read Genesis 1:26-31 and Genesis 2:15. What are our duties to the earth according to God?

10. What was the Once-ler's main character flaw? What do you consider to be the chief cause of sin? See I Timothy 6:10.

(Contributed by Barry DeShetler, Cincinnati, Ohio)

ATHEIST ROLE PLAY

This is a simple discussion starter that deals with the question "Does God Really Exist?" Sometimes it's a good idea to force kids to think through their reasons for believing in God (if they say they do) and to strengthen those beliefs. In addition, it is important to take kids a step further and help them to see how their belief (or non-belief) in

God makes a difference in the way they live.

Begin with a role play. Have the kids pair off. One person takes the role of an atheist (a person who does not believe in God) and the other is a believer. For about three minutes have the kids assume these roles and try to convince the other person that their view is the correct one. After they have done this, have another person (like one of the youth sponsors) come before the entire group and take the position of an atheist. The group must try to convince him that he is wrong. Since the kids have had some practice in their individual role plays, they should be well equipped to do so.

The next step is to give the kids pencil and paper, and to ask them to write down five things that would change in their lives if they knew for certain that there was no God. What difference would it make in the way they lived? Next, have them write down five things that would probably change in their lives if they knew for a fact that there really was a God. In other words, how would their lives be different from the way they are now if God somehow made himself known (by appearing in the sky, or something like that) so that there was absolutely no doubt whatsoever that He existed. How would they behave differently?

Now have the kids compare their lists and discuss the differences between both lists and the way they live right now.

Follow this up with a discussion. Some possible questions:

1. On the basis of arguments presented, etc., do you believe in God or not? (You might have a vote, secret ballot if you want.)
2. Is it possible to "abstain" in a vote for or against the existence of God? In other words, can a person just not have an opinion? What are the consequences of such a position?
3. How does how you believe affect the way you live right now?

(Contributed by Ken Potts, La Grange, Illinois)

BIGGER AND BETTER TALENT HUNT

This is a game that can lead into a learning experience based on the Parable of the Talents (Matthew 25:14-30). The game is the "Bigger and Better Hunt" (previously described in *IDEAS Number Four*).

Begin by dividing into groups of three or four per group. Then give each group a certain amount of money. It could be a penny, or it could be a dollar. The amount doesn't matter too much. The task of each group is to go into the neighborhood and try to trade the money for something of value, and then to continue trading with the purpose of increasing the value each time. In other words, they might begin by going to someone's house and asking them if they had anything that they would be willing to sell (or trade) for the penny (or whatever amount they were starting with). After making the deal, they then go to another house and try to sell that item for more money, or trade it up for something else. The group should have thirty minutes to an hour to work with, and the group that comes back at the end of the time with the most value (either in money or merchandise) is the winner. Kids may not add any of their own money to the total, nor may they solicit donations. The only acceptable method of acquiring more value is through trading.

After the game, follow up with a discussion of what happened. Was it hard to do? How did you approach it? Did some methods work better than others? Did you ever want to just stop at one point and not go any further? Move into a study of the Parable of the Talents and see if the kids are able to understand it better after having played the game. Wrap up with a few thoughts on the importance of taking what God has given to us and putting forth every effort to invest those gifts into meaningful service as opposed to "hiding them under a bushel." Point out that the parable takes the emphasis off of "how many" talents were given and places the emphasis on the amount of effort each person puts into multiplying those talents. (Contributed by Ruth Staal, Grand Rapids, Michigan)

BUT LORD, ISN'T THAT A BIT SHOWY?

Here's a good play on Joshua and the Battle of Jericho that contains a lot of humor and also has a message with some good discussion possibilities.

Characters needed:
1. The Lord
2. Joshua
3. General Beriah
4. Commander Nadab
5. Simeon
6. Ithmar
7. Caleb
8. Horn Player
9. The Curtain (Card bearer)

Hamming up the act is recommended, and costumes can be designed to fit each character. Possibilities are yardstick swords, football or plastic combat hats or saucepans for helmets, with stars on sides for special effect, and so on. Use your own creativity here. You'll also need to make eight cards with the following words written on them:
1. Presenting: But Lord, Isn't That A Bit Showy?
2. Next Day
3. Second Day
4. Third Day
5. Fourth Day
6. Fifth Day
7. Sixth Day
8. Seventh Day

The play begins with all characters in a huddle discussing rather loudly the battle at hand.

Joshua: Alright, men, you know why we're here. We've got to take Jericho. We've been wandering around in the wilderness for forty years and now, finally, we've reached the promised land. But, what happens when we get here? We've got a walled city to conquer. That's why I've ordered all of you to meet with me. I thought we might come up with a plan of attack for capturing Jericho. General Beriah, what do you suggest?

Beriah: Starvation! I think we should surround the city, guard all the roads leading in, and starve them out.

Joshua: That's not a bad idea, General; it has worked before. But, there's a problem. You see, Jericho has a natural spring underneath it to provide them plenty of water. Also, our spies report that there's at least two years of grain supplies in there. I suppose we could sit around here for the next three years, but that seems to lessen our element of surprise. We need to hit fast. In three years they could have the whole Canaanite armies surrounding us. Commander Nadab, what's your idea?

Nadab: I'd like to get some huge trees to use as battering rams and break down the gates. It's a worthy plan, Sir, however . . . there are no trees like that around here. So I don't think it will work.

Ithmar: If only Moses was here.

Joshua: (with irritated glance in Ithmar's direction) Simeon, how about you? You're always ready for battle.

Simeon: I think we should just fight it out. Surround the city and start attacking. If we barrage them long enough and heavy enough with our full weapon power, we'll eventually wear them down.

Joshua: The problem with that, Simeon, is that those walls are so high and wide. We really don't have that many weapons. We need another plan.

Ithmar: I have an idea.

All: (murmuring and nudging each other with smirks) Ithmar has an idea!

Ithmar: I think we should build a large wooden horse, put some men inside, then when they pull the horse into the city the men jump out and open the gates.

Joshua: Ithmar, where did you ever come up with such a thing? How about you, Caleb. What's your idea?

Caleb: Siege work against the city. Then we could go right over the top. Here's how we could do it. Find every basket we can and fill it with dirt. Get our men to carry them right

71

up to the wall and dump them as fast as we can. We'd
have a ramp in no time.

Joshua: That's great!
Lord: Joshua. *(The Lord is offstage; only his voice is heard.)*
Joshua: *(looking around curiously)* Huh? What?
Lord: *(louder)* Joshua!
Joshua: *(moving off by himself)* Uh, just a minute, men. Take ten.
Ithmar: *(annoyed)* I sure wish Moses was here.
Joshua: Yes, Sir?
Lord: What do you think you're doing?
Joshua: We're planning our attack against Jericho, Sir.
Lord: What have you decided?
Joshua: Our ideas? Well, we were going to starve them, then we thought we'd attack them head on. Now we're discussing a possible siege work.
Lord: Did Ithmar contribute an idea?
Joshua: Ithmar? Well, uh, yes Sir. He had this thing about a wooden horse.
Lord: I wonder where he learned to read Greek . . . As Commander-in-Chief, may I make a suggestion?
Joshua: You have an idea for us? Thank you, Lord. Wait a minute, I'll get something to write on. Hey, men, He's got an idea for us! *(pointing up)* Alright, I'm ready.
Lord: First day. Get all the mightiest men together.
Joshua: Right!
Lord: March around the city.
Joshua: Got it.
Lord: Take the rest of the day off.
Joshua: You gotta be kidding?!
Lord: I'm not much of a kidder, Joshua. Second day . . . same thing! Third day . . . same thing. Do that for six days. Then, the seventh day march around the city seven times, shout, and the city's yours!
Joshua: No offense, Lord, but this plan is the pits. We just shout and the whole thing collapses? Lord, I don't know. The men aren't going to believe this. Don't you think that's a bit over dramatic?
Lord: *(clearing throat first)* Joshua, did you have anything to do with the plagues in Egypt?
Joshua: No, Sir, I didn't.
Lord: Did you have anything to do with the parting of the Red Sea?
Joshua: No, Sir, you did it.
Lord: Did you have anything to do with the manna in the wilderness?
Joshua: No, Sir.

Lord:	Do you know how to strike a rock and make water gush forth?
Joshua:	No, Sir. And I didn't have anything to do with the burning bush or parting the waters of the Jordan.
Lord:	I have a reputation for doing things a bit differently, you might say . . . and I'm batting 1000 by the way . . .
Joshua:	*(rolling eyes)* Alright, I get the drift. We'll do it Your way. *(rejoining men)* Okay, men, I've got another plan here.
Ithmar:	I know! We're going to build a giant hollow camel!
Joshua:	NO! Okay? And I wish you'd quit saying, "If only Moses was here." Moses isn't here, but I am and I'm in charge. Moses disappeared up on that mountain and we haven't seen him since. I'm sure he's dead. Anyway, men, here are the orders. In the morning get your best soldiers and equip them with full armor—swords, spears, shields, everything. Have them lined up by dawn. Ithmar, you get the horn act together with your first horn player. We'll be carrying the Arc of the Covenant. We'll march around the city single file, and everyone is to be absolutely quiet. Then, you get the rest of the day off.
All:	*(show signs of disbelief and amazement, some murmuring)*
Joshua:	That's right. The second day we'll do the same thing. Got it? We'll do this six days in a row, then on the seventh day we'll march around the city seven times. While everyone faces the city and the horn plays extra loud, we'll shout and the . . . uh . . . walls . . . will . . . uh . . . tumble down. Now I know it sounds wild, but we're going to do it just like He said. If it doesn't work, it's His fault, not ours. See you in the morning.

(All sack out around the stage. The curtain moves across stage with #2 card. Horn sounds out revelry. Everyone except Ithmar starts getting up.)

Joshua: Okay, everybody up. Let's go. Get in line there. We've got to look in top shape. One time around the city, men. And everyone quiet, except for the blowing of that horn. That *is* a horn, isn't it? Where's Ithmar? *(Ithmar wanders up.)* Ithmar, you slept in.

Ithmar: You know what, Joshua? I think Moses is alive and well and living in the Riviera.

Joshua: ITHMAR! Do you have the horn number ready to go?

Ithmar: *(shrugs shoulders and gets in line)* Yes.

Joshua: *(all marching around a portion of the room)* Okay, let's go. Once around the city. Hup, two, three, four. Keep smiling! All the way around, Ithmar. Blow the horn! Okay, that's it, men. Same time, same place tomorrow.

(The curtain holds up #3 card.)

Joshua: Alright men. Everyone in line. Now, remember, just once around the city.

Beriah: Did you see the way they looked at us yesterday? They hung all over the walls wondering what we were up to.

Joshua: *(talking to himself)* Sometimes I wonder! *(to men)* Now, here we go . . . hup, two, three, four.

(Characters continue to march while the curtain moves across stage showing cards #4 through #8.)

Joshua: *(men stop briefly)* Whew! Well, men, this is it. This is our big day. I hope you're in shape. Seven times around the city, but keep it quiet. Horn, your big number is on the seventh lap. Then everyone turns, shouts, and watches. Alright men, keep in step. Hup, two, three, four. Hup, hup, hup, hup. That's once. Keep it up. Hup, hup. Play that horn! That's twice . . . and three times. Four times. Five . . . Six . . . Seven times. Alright, let her rip! Everyone shout! *(All shout)* It worked! . . . uh, CHARGE! men. Take the city! Ithmar, did you see that?

Lord: Joshua!

Joshua: *(looking up)* Huh? Oh! Go on, Ithmar. *(waves him offstage)* Yes, Sir! Did you see that? It's amazing. What a great plan!

Lord: Joshua, cool your heels, and get this down.

Joshua: Oh, why yes, Sir. I'll write it down.

Lord: Total, strict obedience to the Lord produces amazing, dramatic effects.

Joshua: That's great. Thank you, Lord. I won't forget that, no Sir!

Lord: Well, they don't call me Omnipotent for nothing. And uh, Joshua, tell Ithmar that Moses is up here with me.

Joshua: *(with wide grin and then a glance toward exit)* Ithmar! Hey, Ithmar, I've got news . . .

(Contributed by Marilyn Pfeifer, Washington C.H., Ohio; adapted from an article written by Stephen Bly)

CHRIST IN THE MARKET PLACE

Here's a great program idea that can help kids to think about and experience the fact that Christ is not just for Sunday, but can and should be found in our everyday lives, even in the bustling marketplace.

Have the group meet at the church at a predetermined time. At that time the youth leader gives a short recitation on the idea that Christ should be present in every sphere of life, no matter where you are or what you are doing. The kids are then transported to a large shopping mall. At the mall, they are free to do whatever they want for a certain period of time. They may shop, ice skate, eat, or just mess around. At the end of the time, the kids are to get together and head back to the church.

The instructions that are given to the youth before they go into the mall are these: While they are at the mall they are to look for evidences of Christ in the midst of that busy place. They might find him in stores (paintings of Christ, sculpture, books), or on people (who have crosses around their neck, etc.). Kids are given pencil and paper so that they can jot these things down.

When the kids get back to the church, or whenever you choose to have a meeting for discussion of follow-up on this activity, the kids talk about their findings in the shopping mall. This can be done in conjunction with a discussion of Christ in the marketplace. You'll be surprised to discover how observant the kids can be, and how many different ways they can recognize the presence of Christ in a place that's not considered to be very "sacred." The quote below by George McLeod sums up the point of this discussion. It might be a good idea to give each young person a copy of this quotation to hang up in his/her room.

> "I simply argue that the cross be raised again at the center of the marketplace as well as on the steeple of the church. I am recovering the claims that Jesus was not crucified between two candles, but on a cross between two thieves; on the town garbage heap; at a crossroad so cosmopolitan that they had to write His title in Hebrew and in Latin and in Greek; at the kind of a place where cynics talk smut, and thieves curse, and soldiers gamble. Because that is where He died, and that is what He died about. And that is where the church ought to be, and what the church should be about." —George McLeod, a Scottish Presbyterian Minister

(Contributed by Ron Scates, San Antonio, Texas)

CLIQUES AND LONERS

Here is a program idea that can get kids talking about the effects of "cliques" on a youth group. Ahead of time, arrange the chairs of the youth group and let kids know as they come in that the chairs are not to be moved. Here is how the chairs should be set up, and the people they represent:

1. *A group of chairs in a circle all hooked together:* the group of regular teens who attend the youth group.
2. *A chair in the middle of the circle:* the person who wants to be the center of attention.
3. *A few chairs outside the group:* visitors to the youth group who can't seem to break through and be a part of the group in the circle.
4. *A chair next to the door:* a brand new person who has just entered the group.
5. *A chair outside the door, looking in:* someone waiting to enter the youth group who is afraid to come in.
6. *A chair up on top of the table:* a person who criticizes and looks down on everyone else.
7. *A broken chair or a chair that's different from all the others:* a person in the group who may be a little bit different from the rest because of a handicap, a foreign accent, etc.
8. *A small cluster of 3-4 chairs off from the large circle:* that group of people who stick together and won't let anyone into their group.

You can probably think of some other ways to represent various groupings within a group, and you should try to arrange it so that everyone has a chair, and there are no chairs left over. As the group arrives, give each person a number at random and instruct them to sit in the chair that has the same number. Then, during the meeting you can have a discussion on cliques using the questions below. Everyone must stay in the seats that they have been assigned during the entire meeting.

During the meeting, you could interview (in front of the group) certain kids who are part of established cliques, and also interview someone who is considered to be a "loner." You'll need to be sensitive here. But you could compare the experiences of the kids and try to examine what the problems are, and how they can be solved without destroying relationships or forcing people to do something they cannot do. Here are a few discussion questions that could be tossed out to the group:

1. What is a clique?
2. What are the advantages or disadvantages of being in a clique?

3. What are the advantages or disadvantages of being a loner?
4. What would be the ideal situation in a youth group such as ours?
5. If Christ were in our group, where would He sit? Would He be in a clique? Or would He be a loner?
6. Discuss the ways we as Christians can reach out to loners, or how we can develop positive groupings within our youth group.

(Contributed by Donna McElrath, Upper Marlborough, Maryland, and Carter Hiestand, Augusta, Georgia)

COLORADO OR NEW YORK?

This is an exercise that is fun to do and gets people to think about who they are and what they value. It is also a good community-builder as it helps to open a group up to each other in a non-threatening way.

Print up and pass out the "I AM MORE LIKE. . ." list (below) to each person asking them to circle one word after each number that they feel they are most like (not that they would rather be). Tell them to circle the one they would most often feel like or choose. Ask them to think of the analogy between each of the two items, or of what connotations it would bring to their minds as they try to decide between the two. Explain that one item is not necessarily better than the other, only different.

For example, on item #1, the choice is between Colorado and New York. These two places bring to mind two distinctive environments or personalities. The idea on this one is not necessarily to choose your favorite place, or which one you would rather visit, but which one you are most like. Maybe you are "most like" New York because you have a lot of things going on in your life, or because you are loud and boisterous, or because you are an exciting person. Or you may be more like Colorado, because you see yourself as quiet and alone, or majestic and solid (like the Rocky Mountains), or as clean, uncluttered, or refreshing. Got the idea?

Here is the list to be distributed to the group:

I AM MORE LIKE. . .

1. Colorado. . .New York
2. Volkswagen. . .Mercedes Benz
3. A leaky faucet. . .an overflowing dam
4. Moonlight. . .Firelight
5. Led Zepplin. . .Kenny Rogers

6. The Mountains. . .The Desert
7. Marathon runner. . .Sprinter
8. Silk. . .Flannel
9. Dove. . .Eagle
10. Tug boat. . .Sailboat
11. Easy chair. . .Wood bench
12. Oil Painting. . .Snapshot
13. River. . .Lake
14. Paved highway. . .Rocky road
15. Hand. . .Eye
16. Lock. . .Key
17. Filing cabinet. . .Bulletin board
18. Tire. . .Steering Wheel
19. Arrow. . .The Bow
20. Music. . .The Dancer
21. Collector. . .Dispensor
22. Golfer. . .Sky Diver
23. Checkbook. . .Treasure Chest
24. Social worker. . .Business executive

25. House. . .Tent	31. Cream Cheese. . .Hot Sauce
26. Fall. . .Spring	32. Comedian. . .Lawyer
27. Jaguar. . .Snail	33. Coal. . .Diamond
28. Violin. . .Trumpet	34. Lamb. . .Fox
29. Morning. . .Evening	35. News Report. . .Soap Opera
30. Wax. . .Rock	36. Politician. . .Philosopher

After everyone has completed the exercise, go over each number and have the kids raise their hands if they feel they are more like the first item than the second. Then have those who feel they are more like the second item also raise their hands. Have them discuss the analogies they saw between the two items, and give them the opportunity to share why they picked the item they did.

Some questions for further discussion:

1. Do you ever feel threatened when you discover that your values are different from someone elses? Why? Do you think that God wants us to all have the same values, tastes, personalities, and so forth?
2. Do you think that some of the choices on the list have a "more Christian" response than others?
3. How did your interpretation of the items on the list make a difference in which one you chose? What does this say to us about the value of communication, and trying to understand each other better? Can another person's interpretation be just as right as your own? What does interpretation and first impressions have to do with the way we accept and relate to others?

4. After this exercise, are there certain items that you would like to change? Are you unsatisfied with how you see yourself right now? What can a person do to change?
5. How does our own self-awareness (how we see ourselves) affect the way we relate to others? How we relate to God?

(Contributed by Anna Hobbs, Santee, California)

COUNTING THE COSTS

Load your kids up and drive to the nearby building in the community that was started and never completed. If possible, tour the building grounds and the inside. Ask the group to share possible reasons why the building was never completed. Conclude this part by asking, "What do you think of the contractors?" or "What do the people passing by in this community think?"

Then, read Luke 14:25-30. Discuss how it relates to the unfinished building. Talk about commitment and how to avoid starting something that you can't complete, or not finishing something that you have started. Discussion can also center around what it means to be disciples and what costs there are to be a disciple of Jesus Christ. (Contributed by Doug Newhouse, Florence, Kentucky)

CREATION, GOD, AND YOU

This exercise and discussion is great for camps and retreats, but it can be used almost anywhere. Begin by giving each person a piece of paper and pencil. Take them outside and have them list all the things they notice about nature—the things it does or is like. (For example, the great variety of colors, the intricacy of plant structure, the sun that heats the earth, enabling life to exist, and so on.)

When the time is up, have the group return and share their results with the rest of the group. After this, ask them to describe the most scenic spot they have ever visited or where they think the most beautiful place in the world is, or what it is about creation that amazes them the most. Use this as a take-off to find out what Scripture has to say about God who created it all.

Have different people read the following passages:

Genesis 1:4, 1:26, 2:7   Hebrews 11:3
Romans 1:19-20, 8:21-23   Revelation 4:1

After each passage, have someone briefly state in their own words, what the basic idea of the passage was.

Lead the group in discussion, using the following questions as a way of getting at God's character expressed through His creation. Tell the group to use the Scripture just read and other Scripture as a basis from which to think about and answer the questions.

1. What are some things we know about God upon observing His creation? Can you list some of His attributes?
2. Is creation an extension of God or is creation something separate from God?
3. In the beginning God looked at creation and said it was good Is it still good? Did the "Fall" make it bad?
4. What is the purpose of creation?
5. Is creation still going on? Is God still involved in His creation? Explain.
6. How does creation speak to us in a personal way? Can you name some things that would be relevant to your own personal situation? How does our knowledge of God through creation help us to trust Him?

(Contributed by Anna Hobbs, Santee, California)

THE CRUTCH WALKERS

The following parable is based on the idea that to some people Christianity is only a "crutch." Read it to the group and then discuss the questions that follow.

There existed a planet on which all the inhabitants were unable to walk. They crawled through life not knowing the pleasure of viewing life upright with the easy mobility of walking. History said that many years before the descendants had been able to use their legs effectively and walk upright without crawling or pulling their bodies with their hands as they did now.

One day a person came among them who showed great love and compassion toward them. He told them that not only had their descendants walked on their legs, but that this was possible for them too. He offered crutches for those who believed him, with the promise that someday, if they trusted him, by using their crutches they would be able to walk upright even without them.

Some of the people decided to try the crutches. Once they were upright they found how much larger their world became because of this new ease in mobility. They encouraged everyone to join them in this new found freedom.

Others doubted the crutch walkers would ever be free of their crutches and be able to walk alone. They scoffed at them and said, "We are satisfied with life as we live it. We don't need the assistance of a crutch to experience life. Only the weak need the aide of crutches to get around!"

Questions for discussion:

1. If you were one of the people in the story, would you have tried the crutches? Why or why not?

2. Why do you think some people did not want to try the crutches, and put other people down who did?
3. Do you feel that Christianity is only a "crutch?" If so, in what way? Is this good or bad?
4. How would you respond to a person who rejected Christianity because they thought that it was "only a crutch?"

You might wrap up with some thoughts on the importance of realizing that we are in fact handicapped without Christ, and that it is only when we admit that we are crippled that we are able to walk. Some applicable Scripture might include II Corinthians 12:10, Numbers 21:4-9, John 3:14-16, and John 1:9-12. (Contributed by Bill and Sheila Goodwin, Kalamazoo, Michigan)

DATING QUIZ

Here's a good quiz that can generate a lot of discussion on the subject of dating. After the group has a chance to finish it, go over each question and compare answers.

Circle the best answer:

As a Christian, I may date. . .
  a. non-Christians
  b. non-Christians, but only casually
  c. non-Christians only if they are unusually attractive
  d. any Christian
  e. only "strong" Christians
  f. "Weak" Christians as a ministry
  g. only unusually attractive Christians

It is "more Christian" to...
  a. play the field
  b. only date one person at a time

It is "more Christian" to. . .
  a. wait for a mate until God brings one into your life
  b. go out "hunting" for one if one does not appear (even attending a school where prospects look good)

It is "more Christian"...
  a. for one's parents to pick his or her mate
  b. for me to pick my own mate
  c. to marry a "computer date"
  d. to marry someone you meet at a church conference

It is "more Christian" to. . .
  a. date for companionship
  b. only date someone you might be "serious" about

Finish the sentence:

When you realize that someone you are dating cares much more for you than you do for them, you should. . .

If, as a Christian, you never have any dates and would like some, you should. . .

My pet peave about dating is. . .

Biblical principles I think apply to dating are. . .

Some lessons I've learned about dating are. . .

Prevalent dating practices which I feel are basically non-Christian are. . .

(Contributed by Dan Mutschler, Chicago, Illinois)

DATING QUIZ II

Here are some more good questions on the subject of dating which could be added to or substituted for the questions in the preceding quiz. Again, the idea is not to get the "correct" answer (note that there is no answer key), but simply to generate discussion.

1. I go on a date because. . .
   a. I like to see the latest movies
   b. I enjoy spending my parents' money
   c. I like being broke Sunday through Friday
   d. It gives me something else to do besides homework

2. I select a date by. . .
   a. seeing if he/she is well dressed
   b. hearing whether he/she is a "fun date"
   c. I want to become romantically involved with he/she
   d. all the above

3. Where I go on a date is determined by. . .
   a. the amount of money I have, or the amount that I want to spend
   b. how far my date will let me
   c. where my parents will let me
   d. where my friends are

4. I do not like to double date because...
   a. I do not like to hear unintelligible noises coming from the back seat
   b. we can never all agree where to go, so we drive around a lot
   c. the "other couple" always has bad breath
   d. one of us has to ride with the other two after one of the dates is dropped off

5. I do not date people my own age because. . .
   a. we have nothing in common
   b. he/she still sucks their thumb
   c. they are "all taken"
   d. it's hard to talk with a gorilla

6. I only date "Christian" people because. . .
   a. we both can say God without becoming embarrassed
   b. he/she may keep their hands off me longer
   c. my parents approve
   d. we can pray on our date

7. I never date the same person twice because. . .
   a. he always goes to the same place
   b. I told him that I don't kiss on the first date
   c. the weather forecast is the same for this weekend
   d. I'm afraid we might get involved

8. I never spend much money on a date because. . .
   a. I am saving it for college
   b. she's not worth it
   c. I spent it all on Wednesday night with the "boys"
   d. it has to last me the rest of the month

9. I do not date because. . .
   a. I have no money
   b. nobody has called
   c. she might say no if I ask
   d. I have a case of terminal zits and donkey breath

10. Dating is fun because. . .
    a. I like to dance
    b. I like to get stepped on
    c. I get to mess around
    d. I get out of the house

TRUE/FALSE

1. You should never hold hands on a date, it may lead to more dangerous things.
2. The boy should ask the parents (preferably the father) for permission to date their daughter.
3. To date someone is to look for a potential marriage partner.
4. You should only date Christian people.
5. I like to date someone because they have a pleasant personality.
6. It does not matter how much money was spent on the date so long as we had a good time.

7. I could feel closer to her if she did not bring her pet doberman with her on our date.
8. I like seeing explicit sexual scenes, both at the movies and in the other cars around us.
9. You should always pray (not prey) on a date.
10. I like having my parents drive us on our date.

(Contributed by Joe Dorociak, Memphis, Tennessee)

DOUBTING GAME

Here's a learning game that is fun to play and which provides lots of discussion and thinking on the subject of doubt. You will have to make your own game board, with spaces large enough to write in. (See game board on next page.)

To play the game, divide the group into teams. Each team throws a die and moves along the game board the appropriate number of spaces, like any other board game. As a team, they must do what the space suggests, rotating team members so that everyone gets involved. If the team is unable to do what the space says, they must move back two spaces (just to sit and wait until the next turn). If they can do what is on the space, then they get to draw a "Growth Card" and do what it says. (You will need to make the Growth Cards also.) Another way to play the game is to divide the cards into good cards and bad cards. If the team is unable to answer, they must draw a bad card. If they are able to answer, they get to pick a good card. Be sure to allow plenty of time for questions, answers, and discussion. The game can take up to two hours.

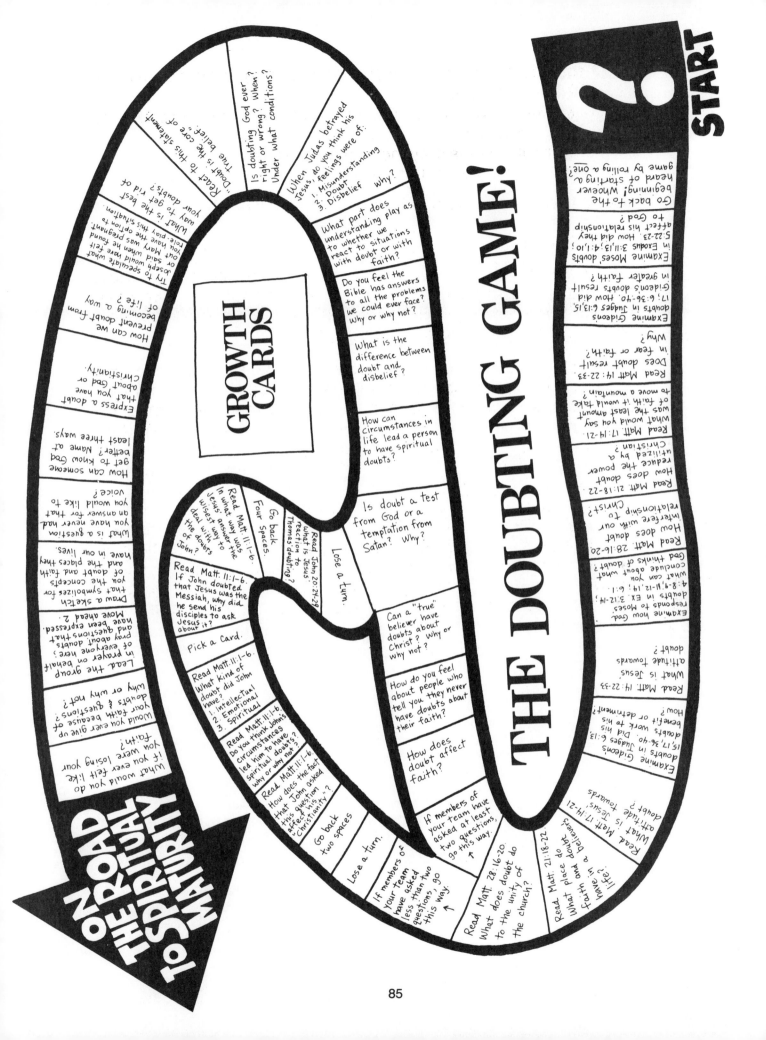

Here are the "growth cards" for the Doubting Game:

If you knew someone with unanswered questions and doubts about Christianity, you would advise him to try another religion. (Move back 3)	It is your opinion that people should keep their questions to themselves. (Move back 2)	You spend time with other Christians to help get you through serious doubts. (Move ahead 2)
Complete faith extinguishes doubt. (Move ahead 1)	You realize that doubt doesn't increase faith, but that faith relinquishes doubt. (Move ahead 3)	Your doubt rules your life. You become too cynical to improve your relationship with Christ. (Move back 3)
You are satisfied with what you "don't know." (Don't move anywhere)	You doubt that God knows what He is doing. (Move back 2)	You have a lot of deep questions about Christianity and you raise them as often as you can. (Move ahead 3)
You believe that God answers prayer. No matter how slowly or how seemingly wrong His answers are. (Move ahead 2)	You think that someone who doubts is just a complainer. (Move back 2)	You expect God's plan to always be so clearcut that there will never be any place for doubting. (Move back 1)
You sometimes doubt your doubts just like you doubt your faith. (Move ahead 2)	Your advice to a doubter is to read his Bible more. (Move ahead 1)	Your doubt gives you a raunchy attitude. (Move back 1)
You feel that doubts give us the desire to learn more. (Move ahead 2)	You discover that emotional doubts are resolved through a change in perspective. (Move ahead 1)	You are able to rise above your doubts and grow spiritually in the midst of them. (Move ahead 3)
You ignore your doubts because you feel they are a sign of unspirituality. (Move back 3)	You realize that God's ways are not our ways, and that we sometimes just have to live with our doubts. (Move ahead 1)	You doubt you will ever understand everything. (Move ahead 2)
You don't usually ask questions because of what others may think of you. (Move back 3)	You realize that doubting is normal and that people who doubt are not weird, dumb, or unspiritual. (Move ahead 3)	You realize that the only way to get answers to hard questions is to ask hard questions. (Move ahead 1)
God tolerates your doubt, but wishes you would mature in your faith. (Move ahead 1)	Your doubts remain, but you are drawn to be more dependent on God as a result. (Move ahead 2)	You feel that the more questions a person has, the more spiritually healthy he is. (Move back 1)
You think that anyone with doubts should question whether he is even a Christian. (Move back 3)	You think doubting is wrong. (Move back 1)	You look forward to the day when you will be able to ask God personally about your doubts and questions. (Move ahead 2)

(Contributed by Jim Walton, Fitchburg, Massachusetts)

EASTER CROSSWORD

Here is a crossword puzzle that tests a group's knowledge of the events leading up to Easter. It can be printed up and done individually, or it can be done as a group game.

Instructions (When done as a group game):

Divide the group into two teams. Teams may elect (or be assigned) to go either "across" or "down." There are an equal number of clues, and it is doubtful that there would be any advantage to being either "across" or "down." There are two (possibly three) rounds in the game. During round one, each team gets a clue (in order) to a word in their section of the puzzle and will get 100 points for each correct answer. The questions (clues) can be given to individuals on the teams, or to the entire team, whichever you decide. Once the answer is given, it cannot be changed, but wrong answers are not written in the puzzle. Alternate questions between the "across" and "down" teams until you have gone through the entire puzzle one time.

During round two, the missed clues are given again in the same fashion, only this time correct answers are worth 50 points. If there are still empty spaces on the puzzle, then go ahead with round three, awarding 25 points for correct answers this time. Also, Scripture references and Bibles may be provided during this round.

A good way to conduct the game would be to make a large poster of the puzzle that could be seen by everyone, or make an overhead transparency of it. Do not give the teams the list of clues in advance.

Clues:

ACROSS

6. Luke's gospel emphasizes Jesus' humanity by calling Him the "_____ of man."
9. This Jewish leader helped prepare Jesus' body for burial (John 19:39).
11. High Jewish priest at the time of the crucifixion (Matthew 26:3).
12. The Jews also wanted to kill this man because he'd been risen from the dead (John 12:10).
13. The man who carried Christ's cross (Luke 23:26).
14. This ripped from top to bottom upon Jesus' death (Matthew 27:51).
18. High council of Jewish leaders (Mark 15:1, NASV, cross-reference).
19. Natural disaster which occurred when Jesus died (Matthew 27:54).
22. Jesus was His only begotten Son (John 3:16).
23. Wealthy Jewish leader who gave His own tomb to Jesus (Matthew 27:59, 60).
26. The "blood money" paid to Judas was eventually used to purchase this burial place for strangers (Matthew 27:6-10).
27. Woman who annointed Jesus with expensive perfume (John 12:3).
28. He caused Judas to betray Christ (Luke 22:3).
29. The disciple who doubted Christ's resurrection (John 20:24, 25).
31. Jesus said He would rebuild this in three days (Mark 14:58).
35. This Old Testament prophet foretold the sufferings of Christ (Isaiah 53).

37. These were fashioned into a crown for Jesus to wear by Roman soldiers (John 19:5).
38. Roman governor who passed the death sentence on Christ (Mark 15:15).
40. The day of Jesus resurrection.
42. Jesus died for _____.
45. Peter was observed in this location when Jesus was taken by the mob (John 18:26).
46. Notorious prisoner released to Jews by Pilate (Mark 15:7-11).
49. Animal which signaled Peter's denial of Jesus (John 18:27).
50. Jesus performed this service for the disciples in the Upper Room (John 13).
51. Gospel writer who devotes the greatest number of chapters to Jesus' last days (John 12-21).
52. Jesus compared His three days in the tomb to the plight of this Old Testament character (Matthew 12:40).
53. He was chosen by lot to replace Judas among the twelve (Acts 1:26).
54. This is a symbol of Christ's body, broken for us (I Corinthians 11:24).
55. The crime which Jesus was accused by the Jews (Matthew 26:65).

DOWN

1. The cry of the multitudes during Jesus' triumphal entry to Jerusalem (Matthew (21:9).
2. Jesus' purpose in going to the Mount of Olives after the Last Supper, to _____ (Luke 22:40, 41).
3. "This is My _____which is given for you; this do in remembrance of Me." (Luke 22:19).
4. Roman soldier at the crucifixion who became convicted of Christ's deity (Mark 15:39).
5. In Gethsemane, Jesus prayed to have this taken from Him (Mark 14:36).
7. Signal used by Judas to betray Christ (Matthew 26:49).
8. Occupation of the two men hung with Jesus (Matthew 27:38).
10. Type of branches cast before Jesus as He entered Jerusalem (John 12:13).
11. Christian sacrament which began with the Last Supper.
15. These were cast by soldiers to divide Christ's clothes (Mark 15:24).
16. First person to see the resurrected Christ (Mark 16:9, John 20:11-18).
17. _____ pieces of silver, the price paid to Judas (Matthew 26:15).

20. "The place of a skull" (where Jesus was crucified) (Mark 15:22).
21. Peter cut an ear off this slave of the high priest (John 18:10).
24. Disciple who denied Christ three times (Luke 21:61).
25. Book of Bible which records Jesus' ascension to heaven (Acts 1:9).
26. The "Feast of Unleavened Bread" (Mark 14:1).
30. Jesus was made to be this for us, that we might become righteous (II Corinthians 5:21).
32. Jesus' crucifixion was part of God's _____ of salvation.
33. The resurrected Jesus appeared to two men on the way to this village (Luke 24:13-15).
34. Christ did this for the bread and wine (Luke 22:17, 19).
36. Setting of the Last Supper (Luke 22:12).
39. Animal which was sacrificed at the Feast of Unleavened Bread (Mark 14:12).
41. Roman soldiers dressed Jesus in this garment of scarlet and mocked Him (Matthew 27:28).
42. Young follower of Jesus (later a gospel writer) who ran away without his clothes when he was seized by the mob in the garden (Mark 14:51, 52).
43. The king of Judea who was in Jerusalem at the time of the crucifixion (Luke 23:8-12).
44. Jesus entrusted the care of His mother to this man (John 19:26, 27).
47. Animal which carried Jesus on His entry to Jerusalem (John 12:15).
48. Name for Jesus which means "teacher" or "master" (Mark 14:45).

(Contributed by Barbara Martin, Delta, Ohio)

EASTER I.Q. TEST

Here is a great little quiz that can be used in conjunction with a Bible study on Easter, or simply to test a group's knowledge of the Easter story as it is presented in Scripture.

Instructions: Place an "x" on the line if you think the answer is Biblically correct:

1. The woman (or women) who went to the tomb was (or were):
   _____*a. Mary Magdalene and the other Mary*
   _____*b. Mary Magdalene, Mary the mother of James, & Salome*
   _____*c. Mary Magdalene, Mary the mother of James, Joanna & others*
   _____*d. Mary Magdalene*

2. The time of early morning was:
   _____*a. when the sun had risen*

_____b. while it was still dark

3. At the tomb was (or were):

_____a. an angel

_____b. a young man

_____c. two men

_____d. two angels

4. The reaction of the woman (or women) was one of:

_____a. amazement, astonishment

_____b. fear and trembling

_____c. great joy

5. After leaving the tomb, the woman (or women):

_____a. told the disciples

_____b. said nothing to anyone

6. The reaction of the disciples at first was that:

_____a. they did not believe the women; it seemed an idle tale

_____b. Peter & John went immediately & quickly to the tomb

7. Jesus first appeared to the disciples:

_____a. in Galilee, on a mountain

_____b. in an upper room in Jerusalem

8. Jesus seemingly last appeared to the disciples:

_____a. on a mountain in Galilee

_____b. on a mountain in Bethany (or just outside Bethany)

_____c. by the Sea of Tiberias

9. The gift of the Holy Spirit was given to the disciples:

_____a. before Jesus ascended; in the upper room he breathed on them

_____b. after Jesus ascended, on the Day of Pentecost

10. We have many details about the crucifixion and death of Jesus. Which Gospel writer gives the most details about the actual Resurrection of Jesus from the grave? Which one best describes what happened when Jesus rose from the dead?

_____a. Matthew

_____b. Mark

_____c. Luke

_____d. John

The answers are found in Matthew 28, Mark 16, Luke 24, John 20-21, and Acts 1. In questions 1 through 9, all of the choices are correct, and in question 10, none are correct, since none of the Gospels describe the actual Resurrection of Christ; only what happened afterward. Obviously this quiz can open up some good discussion on the differences between the four Gospel accounts and how they can be reconciled to each other. (Contributed by Tim Spilker, Lakeside, California)

EGOFEST

Have a meeting in which everyone is encouraged to come up with songs such as "I am the Sunshine of My Life," "I am So Beautiful Today," etc. They can present skits, speeches, games, all which glorify themselves. This part of the meeting can be a lot of fun if pulled off right. Then wrap the whole thing up with a talk about priorities, ego, self-image, relationships, narcissism, and so on. This moving in one direction and then doing a quick reverse is often very effective, if not used too often. (Contributed by Gary R. Sattler, Glen Ellyn, Illinois)

EGO TALK

This idea would work out well in conjunction with the "Egofest" above. Pass out to each person an equal amount of play money which you could print up for the occasion. At some point during the activity, announce that during the next ten or fifteen minutes, you're absolutely not allowed to talk about yourself. In other words, you must not say any of the following words: I, me, my, mine, etc. If someone catches you saying those words, they may ask you for $1, and you must give it to them. If you run out of money (everyone should start with about $10 or so), then you are not permitted to talk until the time is up. Of course, the object is to try to accumulate as much money as you can. You might want to have an auction afterwards. The experience can be very enlightening, as it is almost impossible to carry on a conversation without talking about yourself. This activity can be done at any meeting, and can be followed up with a discussion on self-esteem and so forth. (Contributed by Bob Ingrem, Lake Whales, Florida)

FALSE WITNESS

Ask one of the prominent members of the church whom the youth see around the church a lot, but they don't actually know him very well, to prepare a sermon of about 10 minutes in length. However, this sermon will be a little different in that it will be full of half-truths and not theologically correct. It should be subtle, though, so as not to appear a blatant lie. See how long it takes your group to disagree with what is being said. In one group where this was done, the man that gave this sermon used Scripture references, taken completely out of context, and finished without any of the youth challenging him. After he finished, we went back over what he had said, and they pointed out things they had disagreed with. When asked why they didn't say so before, the most common reply was, "Because he is an adult, a good Christian and we figured he knew what he was talking about."

Use this as a springboard for a discussion about false teachers and how we determine what the truth really is. Some Scripture references that could be used would be: II Cor. 11:14-15, I John 4:1-6, II Peter 2:1-2, Matt. 24:4-5, 11, 24-25, Judy 4. (Contributed by Pam Bates, Tamuning, Guam)

FRIEND OR FOE

This game is designed to illustrate how we are often influenced in our lives, and how difficult it is to really determine who is giving us good advice and who is giving us bad advice. Have a person waiting outside the door while the room is being set up. Place a variety of obstacles, such as pop bottles, around on the floor so that one would have to avoid them in order to walk across the room. Then blindfold the person waiting outside and bring them in. The object of the game is for the blindfolded person to try to walk from one side of the room to the other without knocking over any of the obstacles.

The blindfolded person must get directions to cross the room (around the obstacles) from others in the room, but he does not know who is a friend and who is foe. There will be both giving instructions. It is up to the person who is trying to cross the room to determine who is giving good advice and who is giving bad advice. Whether or not the person can make it through without knocking over any obstacles depends upon who he decides to listen to. He may decide to listen to no one at all and simply try to make it on his own.

After that person crosses the room, someone else can try if they think they can do better. (Rearrange the room a different way this time.) Afterwards, ask the group questions like these:

1. (To the blindfolded persons): How did you decide whom to listen to?
2. (To the blindfolded persons): How did you feel when you followed a direction and it turned out to be bad advice?
3. (To the "Friends and Foes"): What tactics did you use to keep the person on or off the right course?
4. (To the group): How is this situation like the world around us? In what ways does the world try to influence us? How can we learn to stay on course?

If the group is a large one, it would be best to only have six or so who are the "friends and foes," while the others simply watch the action. This game will provide a lot of laughs, as well as some good learning. (Contributed by Wayne Peterson, Cedar Rapids, Iowa)

FRIENDSHIP NOTES

Here's an idea that can help open up communication lines among members of your group, and also strengthen the community-building process as well. Prepare some "note paper" with letter forms printed on it like the samples below. Include the beginnings of sentences to start a thought, and leave the ending blank, with room to complete the thought after each one. Write in the names of the kids in the group on the salutation part of the letters, so that each person in the group will get one, then pass them out. Allow several minutes for the kids to complete the notes, then collect them and "deliver" them to each person they are written to.

After the kids have had a chance to read their notes, they can read them aloud to the group (optional). Some will be humorous, some will be serious, but they will all lead to better communication among group members. Here are a couple of sample letters (you can write your own):

Dear _____ ,

   Today I was thinking about you and _____

_____

   I hope we can _____

_____

You have been _____

_____

Whenever we are together _____

_____

Let us plan to _____

_____ sometime soon.

Your friend,

_____

Dear_____,

I am glad you are in our Youth Group because _____

_____ .

When we can spend time together why don't we _____

_____ ?

I think that you _____

_____ .

I know that others think you are _____

_____ .

As we look forward to the future _____

_____ .

Your friend,

_____

(Contributed by Anne Hughes, Dickinson, Texas)

GESTAPO

This is a fun game that can also be a great learning experience. It can be played with as few as twenty or as many as five hundred.

The setting is in Poland in 1940. Jews are desperately trying to keep away from the Germans who are trying to put them in concentration camps.

You should have a large playing area with plenty of places to hide. Designate a twenty by twenty square to be the jail for captured people. You will need enough flashlights for your German patrol (you should only have one tenth of your total group be Germans) and some crepe paper arm bands to designate them as Germans. Designate five to fifteen people to be Christians. Give each of them a playing card or something they can place in their pocket so they can be identified. The rest of the group are Jews. This is a night game and should be played for about one hour.

Send the Jews out into the playing area and give them five minutes to do their work. The Christians have a decision to make. They can operate freely on the playing field and not be arrested by Germans unless they are in the company of Jews. If they are with Jews, they are considered in violation of German law and can be sent to the jail. Jews cannot hide by themselves. They must be hiding with a Christian who is willing to take the chance to hide them. One special German should be designated to guard the jail. A whistle is blown and the German patrol is sent out. Jews and Christians with Jews are captured when a German patrol shines a flashlight on them. Germans take captured people back to the jail where they must sit in the uncomfortable area.

At the end of the game there are no real winners. Stop when you feel that the game has peaked. This is a game of survival for the Jews and of decision-making for the Christians. The Christians have to act as they feel a Christian would, knowing that they are bound by the law, and that the Germans are doing what the government requires them to do.

Follow-up with a discussion of what happened, how everyone felt during the game, and try to relate it to life today. How do we determine Christian ethics? When might violence or breaking the law be justified? Is it ever? There are many possibilities for learning from this game.

You may modify the rules for the game in any way you choose, and you might even want to change the name of the game and the names of the racial groups if you feel that some people might be offended. In other words, you might have the Germans be "The Police Force" and the Jews could be any ethnic or religious minority. (Contributed by Terry Hargrave, Amarillo, Texas)

GET A JOB

It is extremely helpful to young people for caring adults to offer guidance in the area of how to select a career and to find employment. One good way to do this is to invite a variety of persons from within your own congregation to come and share their occupations with the youth group. You might want to invite a factory worker, a social worker, an accountant, school teacher, a business man, and your pastor. Just try to get a good cross-section of occupations.

The discussion can then center around the process by which each person came to do that which he/she does, and how being a Christian makes a difference on the job. Each person on the panel can share from their own personal experience and try to offer suggestions to the young people on pitfalls to avoid and so on. This process not only can be very helpful to the kids, but also offers an excellent opportunity for the youth group to get better acquainted with people from the congregation. (Contributed by David Markle, Anderson, Indiana)

GIFTS OF BEAUTY

The following is a short skit that can be used effectively to open up discussion on the concept of "The Body of Christ" or on "Spiritual Gifts," as found in such Scriptures as I Cor. 12. Each participant in the skit should ham up his/her role, and emphasize the part of the body that they are playing. For instance, the eyes could wear some of those giant glasses, and the mouth could use a megaphone, and so on. You might want to label each part with a sign that is worn by the actors.

The script below can be used as it is, or you can add more lines, other parts of the body and create your own dialogue. Follow-up with a discussion based on the subject matter presented.

EAR:	Where is hand when I need him?
EYE:	He's over there picking nose.
EAR:	What! He's always goofing off when I need him!
MOUTH:	What do you need him for anyway?
EAR:	I need him to clean out the wax in me.
HAND:	I don't know why you guys are yelling at me. Look, foot's in mouth!
EAR:	You both are a couple of goof-offs.
EYE:	To be honest, we've all been goofing off a lot lately.
NOSE:	Yeah, look how bad we've made this kid we're on look.
EAR:	I heard the ugliest girl in town turned him down for a

date.

MOUTH:	Thank Goodness! I'd hate to have to kiss *her* goodnight!
FEET:	Does anybody know how we can help him look better?
EYE:	I was reading the Bible the other day and it said that everyone has a spiritual gift. Maybe if we all find our spiritual gifts we can make this kid look a lot better.
EVERYBODY:	Yeah! Let's go!

(SOME LENGTH OF TIME LATER)

EYE:	Well, did everybody find their gifts?
EVERYBODY:	Yeah!
NOSE:	My gift is to smell all of the wonderful things God has made.
EYE:	My gift is to read the Scriptures and to see the good in others.
EAR:	My gift is to hear the sounds of nature and the voices of people.
MOUTH:	My gift is to tell others about God.
HAND:	My gift is to help other people.
FEET:	My gift is to take us places where we can use our gifts.
EYE:	I'm sure glad I found my gift!
NOSE:	Me, too! I was getting tired of running anyway.

(Contributed by Shane Jent, Bloomington, Illinois)

HANDICAPPED

The following exercise is designed to help young people to better identify with the problems and feelings of the handicapped in our society. Instruct the group to read the situation below and then to complete the questions that follow, answering each one as honestly as they can. Discuss each question with the entire group and try to apply the learning that takes place to your local situation and to those people who may be handicapped in some way.

The Situation: Imagine that you have been transported to another society in another time and place. People look the same, dress the same, but something very important is different: the way they communicate. All people communicate by telepathy, that is, the direct transfer of thoughts from one person's mind to another. They are carrying on normal lives, enjoying each other, working, playing, going to school, but you have a serious problem—you cannot give or receive telepathic messages. People seem shocked that you are unable to communicate; some avoid you, some even make fun of you. You can communicate if you are able to write messages out, but very few people care to take the time to converse in this manner. Unable to find work and support yourself, you go to the local government for help. After waiting in line for an hour and being referred to several different departments, you are finally instructed to apply for admission to a mental institution for the non-telepathic, and begin therapy immediately.

1. How would you feel about the people of this world?

2. How would these experiences make you feel about yourself?

3. How would you feel about the government of this world?

4. Would you go to the institution for therapy or not? If not, what would you do instead?

5. If you came upon a Christian church in this world, how would you expect the people there to respond to your situation?

6. How would you feel about someone who took the time to learn to communicate with you and became your friend?

(Contributed by Jim Steele, Lake Oswego, Oregon)

HANDICAPPED

At a week-night fellowship, let the kids know that they're about to take part in a fascinating learning experience. Pass out various forms of bandages, slings, eye-patches, crutches, dark glasses, etc. (You might even challenge some of the kids to walk with a limp, feign blindness, or ride in a borrowed wheelchair.) Divide them into twos (one healthy and one "handicapped") and with a van, drop them off at various spots around the area; i.e. shopping centers, restaurants, stores, etc. for a certain period of time. (The leader will need to have that well-planned.) After regrouping, an interesting discussion is sure to arise about the plight and feelings of the handicapped, prejudices against the weak or strange appearing, etc. Have some Scriptures on hand to investigate God's guidance on these things. (Contributed by Mark Wesner, Ft. Wayne, Indiana)

HELLO GOD, WHERE ARE YOU?

Here is an idea to help your youth group to get in touch with God in a personal way, enabling them to see how God works in their own lives.

Begin by having each person write down a few ways that they have actually experienced God's active involvement in their lives during the last week or two. These can then be shared with the entire group. You might also ask the kids to write down some barriers in their lives that have kept them from experiencing God's involvement in their lives. These can also be shared and discussed.

After this discussion, introduce the idea of keeping a journal as a way of helping us to overcome some of these barriers and to notice God's activity in our lives. A journal is a type of diary in which the kids write down (everyday, or whenever possible) their insights, observations, questions, discoveries, and so on.

You can provide inexpensive spiral notebooks for use as a journal or the kids can come up with their own. Have each person choose one or more of the following journal formats which would be most appropriate to his/her own personal needs. Also decide on a time span for this journal keeping period. It could be a week, a month, or even longer. Each person should include the date on each entry, although they do not have to be done every day. However, in order for it to be effective, it should be written in at least twice a week. Here are some possible formats:

1. *Insights:* The focus here is on being aware of the relationship between our faith, things around us, and the experiences we have. Whenever something happens that makes you aware of your relationship to God, or if you see Him at work in your life, you should write it down as it comes to you.

2. *Questions and Searchings:* Write down the questions that you have each day or week, the things that bothered you, challenged you, that seemed to cause conflicts, that made you wonder. Look for those things you would like to understand better and write down these things as you review your day or week.

3. *Thanksgivings:* Write down each day two or three things that gave you reason to celebrate, to be happy about, or that you were thankful for.

4. *Meditations:* The focus here is on making Scripture real and practical. Read a passage of Scripture each day (this could be pre-assigned) and write down the verse that sticks in your mind from that day. Write below it 3 or 4 ways you could apply it that day or week.

5. *Self-Motivation:* Write down a goal for the week at the top of the page. You might want to look for a verse in Scripture that would help encourage or support you in accomplishing this goal. Write down 3 or 4 ways you could work on your goal during the coming

week. A self-evaluation blank at the bottom of the page could be included so that you can keep a record of how you are doing towards attaining that goal. Make the goals simple, specific, and attainable.

6. *Prayers:* Write out prayer requests, leaving a space below or beside the request. When the prayer is answered, you can write the date in the space.

You may want to keep in touch with the kids personally during this journal keeping period to encourage them and to see how they are doing. At the end of the time period, get together with the group so that you can share and reflect on some of the things that they've learned, struggled with, or become more aware of while keeping their journals. Some kids may want to continue keeping their journals long after this experience. Those who are unable to follow through with the journal can share why it was difficult for them. (Contributed by Anna Hobbs, Santee, California)

HOW MANY F'S?

Here is a fun little experiment that can be tied in quite nicely with a lesson on awareness. Print up some sheets like the one below and give one to each person in the group face down. Everyone turns the page over and begins at the same time. Each person should work alone.

Read the following sentence in the enclosed block. After reading the sentence, go back and count the F's. You have <u>one</u> minute.

```
┌─────────────────────────────┐
│  FINISHED FILES ARE THE RE- │
│  SULT OF YEARS OF SCIENTIF-  │
│  IC STUDY COMBINED WITH      │
│  THE EXPERIENCE OF YEARS.    │
└─────────────────────────────┘
```

Number of F's in the block _____

Try it yourself before you read the answer below.

Most people will count three. Others will see four or five. Only a few will count all six F's that are in the box. After the 30 seconds are up, ask the group how many F's they counted, and you will get a variety of answers. Those who counted only three, four, or five will be quite surprised when you tell them the answer. But after they find all six F's, they will feel rather silly that they didn't see them in the first place. Most people tend to overlook the word "OF" when they are counting. This is because they are looking only at the bigger words.

This test is often given to people in driving classes to demonstrate how we often fail to see motorcycles on the road because they are so small, and because we aren't looking for them. After they are pointed out, they become obvious. This lesson can also be applied to people. We often miss the good qualities in other people because we aren't looking for them. We tend to look instead for the things that we want to see—the bad things. This is to make ourselves look good by comparison.

Follow up on this idea with an exercise like "What Others Think Of Me" (in *IDEAS Number Eleven*) in which kids look for the good in each other, and affirm each other's gifts and abilities. It's amazing how when these things are pointed out, they then become more obvious. It also does a lot for everyone's self-esteem.

HUMAN SLIDE SHOW

Here's a nifty way to present a Bible passage or story. Break your group into different groups and give each one a Scripture passage. Each group is to pretend they're presenting a slide show of the passage given. The story is divided into different "slides" to illustrate the story. Each "slide" will have the members of the group in a still-life pose to depict each scene. As one person in the group narrates, the group poses in each "slide" at the appropriate time in the story. A parable can be broken into 4 to 8 slides. This idea not only teaches a Bible story, but it's loads of fun. If you have a devotion planned, the Human Slide Show is an excellent method of presenting the Scripture passages you will use. (Contributed by Milton Hom, Richmond, California)

IDENTITY MASKS

Get some large grocery sacks. Cut out a slot in each sack for the eyes so that it might be used as a mask over the head. On the sacks, write (in red) different identities adolescents get in high school. Under these names, write down (in black) how they are to be treated.

Give each person one of these masks, face down so that they don't know what is on it. Have the kids shut their eyes and put the masks on for them so they cannot see who they are. Tell them to mill around the room and interact with each other. They have two tasks: to treat each person according to the directions on the masks, and to guess who they are from the interaction of others with them. Tell them to keep in touch with their feelings, especially their feelings about themselves. (For best results: give the negative labels to the most outgoing, accepted kids in the group and the positive labels to the quieter, less noticed ones.)

Here are some ideas for masks (be creative with others):

Joe Cool *-ask me to parties*
  -accept me
  -laugh at all I say
  -tell me how cool I am

Patty Party *-invite me to any social gathering*
  -accept me
  -act wild and uninhibited around me

Betty Bod *-ask me out*
  -accept me
  -flirt with me
  -tell me how good looking I am

Jerry Jock *-tell me how strong I am*
  -talk about sports around me
  -flirt with me
  -ask me to be on your sports team

Ivan Intellect *-respect me for my "smarts"*
  -ask me to sit by you in class
  -tell me how intelligent I am

Steven Stud *-ask me out*
  -tell me how good looking I am
  -flirt with me
  -accept me—get in good with me

Bryan Bookworm *-reject me*
  -tell me I'm boring
  -poke fun at me

Ralph Runt *-kid me about being small*
  -reject me subtly
  -act big around me

Andy Clutz *-reject me*
  -tell about the dumb things I do
  -tell a joke about me

Paul Problem *-feel sorry for me*
  -tell me how you understand
  -ask me if it's going better today
  -don't respect me

Susie "Dumb" Blonde *-treat me as spacy*
  -but flirt with me

Nelson Nerd   *-reject me*
              -make nasty remarks to me
              -make fun of me

Wanda Wallflower   *-reject me—don't acknowledge me*
                   -don't speak to me even if I talk

Ms. Liberation   *-accept me*
                 -tell me how good I am in sports
                 -act free around me
                 -but don't ask me out or tell me I'm pretty

Ted Tough Guy   *-act afraid of me*
                -ask me if I've heard any off-color jokes lately
                -try to get on my good side
                -ask me to help you "get even" with somebody

After the kids have had a chance to mingle long enough for their new personalities to form, discuss how who we are comes from others' opinions of us. Discuss also how labels are not our real selves—people try to hang their trips on us. Then show God's view of us and how His opinion of us is the one which should shape our lives. (Contributed by Gary Salyer, Anderson, Indiana)

IF GOD SHOULD SPEAK

Sometimes we say the Lord's Prayer so often that it becomes meaningless. The following skit is a great way to alert people to the fact that God is listening to our prayers, even when we pray the Lord's Prayer, and just may have something to say to us if we listen to Him when we pray.

The person who is praying should memorize his or her lines so that the dialogue sounds natural rather than stiff, and the person doing the voice of God (offstage, out of view) could read God's part. Plenty of rehearsal will add a great deal to the impact.

Follow-up this presentation with a discussion on the two-way communication that should exist in prayer, and you may also want to discuss some of the issues raised in the skit itself.

Introduce the skit to the audience by saying, "Prayer is a dangerous thing. You could wind up with some major changes in your life..."

The Script:

"Our Father which art in heaven . . ."
> *Yes.*

Don't interrupt me. I'm praying.
> *But you called me.*

Called you? I didn't call you. I'm praying. "Our Father which art in heaven . . ."
> *There, you did it again.*

Did what?

> *Called me. You said, "Our Father which art in heaven." Here I am. What's on your mind?*

But I didn't mean anything by it. I was, you know, just saying my prayers for the day. I always say the Lord's Prayer. It makes me feel good, kind of like getting a duty done.
> *All right. Go on!*

"Hallowed be thy name . . ."
> *Hold it! What do you mean by that?*

By what?

> *By "Hallowed be thy name?"*

It means . . . it means . . . Good grief! I don't know what it means! How should I know? It's just part of the prayer. By the way, what does it mean?
> *It means honored, holy, wonderful.*

Hey, that makes sense. I never thought what "hallowed" meant before. "Thy kingdom come, thy will be done, on earth as it is in heaven."
> *Do you really mean that?*

Sure, why not?

> *What are you doing about it?*

Doing? Nothing, I guess. I just think it would be kind of neat if you got control of everything down here like you have up there.
> *Have I got control of you?*

Well, I go to church.

> *That isn't what I asked you. What about that habit of lying you have? And your temper? You've really got a problem there, you know. And then there's the way you spend your money . . . all on yourself. And what about*

104

the kind of books you read?

Stop picking on me! I'm just as good as some of the rest of those people—those phonies—at church!

Excuse me! I thought you were praying for my will to be done. If that is to happen, it will have to start with the ones who are praying for it. Like you, for example.

Oh, all right. I guess I do have some problems, some hang-ups. Now that you mention it, I could probably name some others.

So could I.

I haven't thought about it very much until now, but I really would like to cut out some of those things. I would like to, you know, be really free.

Good! Now we are getting somewhere. We'll work together, you and I. Some victories can truly be won. I'm proud of you!

Look, Lord! I need to finish up here. This is taking a lot longer than it usually does. "Give us this day, our daily bread."

You need to cut out some of that 'bread'. You're overweight as it is.

Hey, wait a minute! What is this, "Criticize Me Day?" Here I was, doing my religious duty, and all of a sudden you break in and remind me of all my problems and shortcomings.

Praying is a dangerous thing. You could wind up changed, you know. That's what I'm trying to get across to you. You called me, and here I am. It's too late to stop now. Keep on praying. I'm interested in the next part of your prayer. . . (pause)—Well, go on!

I'm afraid to.

Afraid? Afraid of what?

I know what you'll say next.

Try me and see.

"Forgive us our trespasses, as we forgive those who trespass against us."

What about Joe?

I knew it! See, I knew you would bring him up! Why, Lord, he's told lies about me, and cheated me out of some money, and is the biggest phoney around. He never paid back that debt he owes me. I've sworn to get even with him and then never associate with him again!

But your prayer! What about your prayer?

I didn't mean it.

Well, at least you're honest. But it's not much fun carrying that load of bitterness around inside you, is it?

No, but I'll feel better as soon as I get even. Boy, have I got some plans for old Joe! He'll wish he never did me any harm.

> *You won't feel any better. You'll only feel worse. Revenge isn't sweet. Think of how unhappy you are already. But I can change all that.*

You can? How?

> *Forgive Joe. Then the hate and sin will be Joe's problems, not yours. You may lose the money, but you will have settled your heart.*

But Lord, I can't forgive Joe.

> *Then how do you expect me to forgive you?*

Oh, you're right! You always are! And more than I want revenge on Joe, I need to be right with you. All right, I forgive him. Lord, you help him to find the right road in life. He's bound to be awfully miserable now that I think about it. Anybody who goes around doing the things he does to others has to be out of it. Someway, somehow, show him the right way. Maybe you can even help me to help him?

> *There now! Wonderful! How do you feel?*

Hmmm! Well, not bad. Not bad at all. In fact, I feel pretty great! You know, I don't think I'll have to go to bed uptight tonight for the first time since I can remember. Maybe I won't be so tired from now on because I'm not getting enough rest.

> *You're not through with your prayer. Go on!*

Oh, all right. "And lead us not into temptation, but deliver us from evil."

> *Good! Good! I'll do that. Just don't put yourself in a place where you can be tempted.*

What do you mean by that?

> *Change some of your friendships. Some of your so-called friends are beginning to get to you. Don't be fooled! They advertise that they're having fun, but for you it could be ruin. Either you are going to have to stop being with them, or start being a positive influence on their lives. Don't you use me as an escape hatch!*

I don't understand.

> *Sure you do. You've done it a lot of times. You get caught in a bad situation. You get into trouble by not listening to me, and then once you do, you come running to me, saying, "Lord, help me out of this mess, and I promise you I'll never do it again." You remember some of those bargains you tried*

to make with me, don't you?

Yes, I do, and I'm ashamed Lord. I really am.

Which bargain are you remembering?

Well, when the woman next door saw me coming out of that X-rated movie with my friends. I'd told my mother we were going to the Mall. I remember telling you, "Oh, God, don't let her tell my mother where I've been." I promised to be in church every Sunday.

She didn't tell your mother, but you didn't keep your promise, did you?

I'm sorry, Lord, I really am. Up until now, I thought that if I just prayed the Lord's Prayer every day, then I could do what I liked. I didn't expect anything like this to happen.

Go ahead, and finish your prayer!

"For thine is the kingdom, and the power, and the glory, for ever. Amen."

Do you know what would bring me glory?
What would make me really happy?

No, but I'd like to know. I want to please you. I know what a difference it can make in my life. I can see what a mess I've made of my life, and I can see how great it would be to really be one of your followers.

You just answered my question.

I did?

Yes. The thing that would bring me glory is to have people like you truly love me. And I see that happening between us now. Now that these old sins are exposed and out of the way, well, there's no telling what we can do together.

Lord, let's see what we can make of me and my life, OK?

Yes, let's see!

(Contributed by Walt Kukkonen, Sterling, Illinois)

IMAGES OF THE CHURCH

The New Testament uses quite a few metaphors to describe the function of the church in the world. These metaphors are used to help us to understand not only who we are as the church, but what our relationship should be to Christ, and to each other.

You might want to begin with a study of each of these "word pictures" of the church, and then have the kids rank order them from most important to least important, or from best to worst. Of course, the idea is not necessarily to imply that any of the metaphors are unimportant or more important than others, but simply to generate a discussion on the subject. You might have the kids think of some additional metaphors, borrowing from modern day culture to create their own images of the church.

Here is a list of metaphors used in the New Testament:

1. *Bride:* we are the bride; Christ is the bridegroom (See II Cor. 11:2, Eph. 5:25, Romans 7:4, Rev. 19:7)
2. *Branches:* Jesus said that He was the vine, and that we are the branches. (See John 15:1-8)
3. *Flock:* Jesus said that we were sheep and that He is the Good Shepherd. (See John 10:11-15. Also see Matthew 10:16)
4. *Kingdom:* Jesus was called the Mighty King, the King of Kings, and that we are brought into His Kingdom. (See Colossians 1:13)
5. *Family:* We are the sons and daughters of God, brothers of Christ, brothers and sisters to each other, joint heirs with Christ, the household of God. (See Hebrews 2:10-11, Galatians 4:1-7)
6. *A Building:* We are temples of the Holy Spirit, a building not made with hands. (See II Cor. 5, Ephesians 2:19-22)
7. *A Body:* We are all part of the Body of Christ, each person being a different part of the body. (See I. Cor. 12, Ephesians 4)
8. *Salt:* We are the salt of the earth. (See Matthew 5:13)
9. *Light:* We are the light of the world. (See Matthew 5:14)
10. *Fishermen:* Jesus called us to be fishers of men. (See Matthew 4:19)
11. *Soldiers:* Fighting against "principalities and powers," wearing the full armour of God. (See Ephesians 6:10-17, Thessalonians 5:8)

(Contributed by J. W. Arroz, Lakeside, California)

LEGALISM STROLL

This is a good exercise that helps young people to understand that a legalist approach to the Christian life is not feasible. It can be used to compare and contrast righteousness under the law and righteousness under grace.

The basic idea is for kids to follow a strip of tape through the church (or whatever area you have available), walking on the tape with both feet, being careful not to leave the "straight and narrow" path. Stationed along the line at various points are numerous "temptations" (set up by the youth sponsors) that are designed to get the kids to leave the line. Some of these can be pleasurable things designed to lure them away, and other things can incorporate the use of scare tactics. Kids are told at the outset that their task is to stay on the tape, and if they do (without ever stepping off of it), there will be a reward for them at the end of the tape.

Temptations along the way can include the following:

1. Someone shooting at them with a squirt gun at a certain point,

making them mad or uncomfortable.

2. The youth director can sit in a chair about twelve feet away from the line, and there can be a pile of water balloons just out of arms' reach of the kids. The youth director dares anyone to try and hit him with a water balloon. (But they have to leave the line in order to do it.)
3. At one point, you can try to persuade kids that you need their help to lure someone else off the line.
4. Someone dressed as a monster can jump out and scare them off the line.
5. Place cookies, punch, candy, etc. on the table just out of reach of the line. Leave the table unattended, but have someone watching from a hidden position.
6. At one point, kids can be told by a youth sponsor that the game has been terminated, that they don't need to follow the line anymore. The whole thing was just a joke and there isn't really a reward for them.

You can think of other ideas for temptations or tactics designed to get them to stray from the straight and narrow. Some of them will work, and some of them won't. There will undoubtedly be some kids who proceed right along the line without leaving it, but many will succumb to temptation somewhere along the way. This will lead into an excellent discussion on the topics previously described. Try to relate the various temptations to actual or real temptations that we face all the time. For example, when they are told that the game is over (when it wasn't), they will cry foul because they were lied to, but this can be tied in with the idea that Satan is a liar. Wrap up with a discussion on the impossibility of living a perfect life (or staying on the line forever), and how Christ has provided us with another, better way. (Contributed by Les Palich, Manhattan, Kansas)

LETTERS TO JESUS

Many young people feel inadequate or awkward when praying out loud in front of a group. They don't do it very often, so they really feel intimidated when they are asked to pray, even though they may want to. This exercise is designed to help overcome some of those fears. Have the group imagine that they are writing a letter to Jesus. Give them pencils, paper, and some idea of what the letter should include.

For example, the letter should begin with greetings and perhaps some thank yous. Thank Him for something personal. Thank Him for someone or something and tell why. Share with Him some experiences you've had lately, when you felt happy, and when you felt lousy. Share with Him some of your concerns and worries. If you have any requests, mention those somewhere in your letter, as well.

After the kids have had time to write their letters, explain that these letters are just like prayers, and that God actually does get them. You might want to go around the groupand share the letters with each other. Of course, kids should be allowed to pass if they want to. You might suggest that reading them out loud (either in the group, or at home privately) is the same as "mailing" the letters. (Contributed by Billy King, Weatherford, Oklahoma)

LETTERS TO MAMA

The following "letters" can be used a variety of ways. One of the most effective would be to use them as the script (or partial script) for a short play. The setting can be the Tarsus home of Saul's (Paul's) mother and family. Each scene involves the receiving of another letter from Saul, with everyone gathering around while "Mama" reads the letter (with a traditional Jewish accent, of course). Use your own creativity if you take this approach.

They can also be read to the group, or printed as a resource for any study on the conversion and life of the Apostle Paul. They add a new dimension to one's perception of Paul as a human being. Possible discussion can center around how "Mama" might have responded to the letters. Or you can compare Paul's experience with the conversion experiences of people today, and how others react to such things.

Dear Mama:

Peace from the God of our Fathers, from your distant son, Saul.

Well, Mama, I arrived safely. The ship sailed smoothly out to Cyprus and we pulled in at Salamis around mid-day. I had plenty of time to visit Aunt Beulah.

By the way, little Elizabeth isn't little any more. She married the potter's son, a fine young man named Clypus. They're expecting their first by Purim. May all their children be boys! That reminds me, if I'm able to come home by Spring I'll bring you some purple linen for sister Maria's wedding present. May she find a husband soon!

From there we travelled down the coast to Joppa. Then, the long journey from the coast up to Jerusalem. By the time we saw the giant walls and magnificent gates, I was too tired to care. I headed straight for the Via Blanco. I recognized Mr. Benarma at once. He had received your letter and warmly welcomed me. His son, Simeon, will attend Gamaliel's classes with me.

After a day's rest I took time to tour the city. What a thrill! Mama, you and Papa must come here some day. Imagine! I stood on the rock where Abraham stood. I saw with my own eyes the tomb of King David. I even touched with my own hands the giant stone blocks of Solomon's temple. Oh, may our eyes see the day when a Lion from the Tribe of Judah reigns and rules in Jerusalem again. Perhaps . . . next year by Passover.

The hatred for the Romans here is ten times worse than in Tarsus. And there are street corner prophets all over the city. I even heard of a strange one out on the Jordan River. I must go out and see him—just for a laugh, of course. He seems to have the knack of making everyone mad at him. Just like the butcher there in Tarsus, right, Mama?

Oh, and I must mention another one. He spends his time mainly up north, around Galilee. We hear rumors of his troublesome teachings. But, don't worry about me. I won't have anything to do with such people. I'm here to learn of the God of our Fathers.

Please tell Papa the standard fees for Gamaliel's classes are more expensive than I thought. I will need to do some work for Mr. Benarma in the tent business to add a little income. If you happen to have an extra denarii or so, I know a poor, hard-working student who could put it to good use.

Give my love to Phineas, Elias, and Challa; also, of course, to Maria and the rest of the family.

Greet one another with a holy kiss.

Your son,
Saul

Dear Mama:

Peace from the Lord of Heaven, and from Saul, your obedient and faithful son.

I hope my long delay in writing to you caused no needless anxiety. I've been busy with studies of the Mikra and Talmud. Oh, Mama, the cloak you sent is beautiful. It fits just right and I wear it every cool day.

A few weeks ago we had some free time, so Simeon and Rabin and I walked out to the Jordan to hear the preacher I told you about. His name's John. What a sight! He wore an old camel skin and ranted like a mad man about King Herod. It didn't surprise me a bit to hear later that he had been arrested and thrown into prison.

Oh, yes, do you remember the one I mentioned from Galilee! Actually, he's a Nazarene—Jesus, by name. He's collected quite a following up north. He's a primitive moral teacher, at best. He has no academic background. Just a carpenter from Galilee. May the Lord of Heaven deliver us from these ignorant troublemakers!

I tell you, Mama, there's a great need for solid traditional teaching. Well, I supposes they'll arrest this one, too. So be it.

Tell Papa I certainly appreciate the ten denarii. Of course, it is all gone by now. But, it did enable me to purchase half of the scrolls I needed. Now, if only I could buy the other half . . .

I send this letter by Benjamin. Please tell me what's going on. He tells me nothing from Tarsus, only about Maria.

Greetings to all my friends.

Your wandering scholar son,
Saul

Dear Mama:

Peace from your son, Saul.

Events here have been moving at a lightning pace. I'm preparing to take a trip to Damascus on official business of the High Priest.

As you can tell, the handwriting is not my own. I'm dictating this letter to my secretary. Yes, I have some staff now. It comes with being Chairman of the Young Pharisees Council in Jerusalem. Most of my studies have been suspended because of the disturbances here. This Jesus of Nazareth—may his soul be in torment forever—kept stirring up the people in the north. We all knew it was just a matter of time until he made his move into Jerusalem.

He came during Passover. First, he convinced the people of Bethany—may God forgive their simple hearts—that he had raised one Lazareth from the dead. Yes, they really believed it. Then, he marched into the city leading an army of followers. He headed straight for the temple and threw all the merchants out.

Later, when I heard there was a reward for information leading to his arrest, I decided to investigate myself. But, my effort was not needed. On the day before Sabbath, Simeon woke me.

"They got him", he said. "They arrested him last night."

We headed for the council. But, to our amazement the trial was over. I still don't know how they did it so quickly. Governor Pilate pronounced a capital punishment verdict and he was crucified with some other outlaws that same day.

The following week Rabin came up to me before class and said, "They claim the Nazarene is alive."

Can you believe it, Mama? People actually claim that a dead man lives again. Well, we all had a good laugh. However, several weeks later some of his followers showed up around town and disturbed the Synagogue services with their wild tales. Not only did they say their master was alive, but they called him our longed for Messiah.

At this point I couldn't restrain myself. The old Tarsus blood boiled. I had no idea the movement could be so blasphemous.

We arrested and imprisoned every follower we could find. We broke up every meeting, disrupted every teaching, and generally chased the whole lot out of Jerusalem.

But, they only spread their lies into the countryside.

I made a personal appeal to the High Priest (we're becoming quite good friends, Mama) and I received permission to travel throughout the area to arrest all I could find. You might say I'm the Chief Investigator.

Please, Mama, don't worry. They're not a violent lot. Usually they don't put up any resistance at all. I figure we'll have the whole mess cleaned up within the year. And it certainly won't hurt my status here in Jerusalem.

Don't expect me to write for awhile. Tell Maria I'm so sorry to miss her wedding. May she be the mother of twelve sons! Benjamin is a good man. Treat him kindly, Mama.

Greet everyone in the love of the Holy One.

Your son,
Saul

Dear Mama:

Grace and Peace to you from God our Father and the Lord Jesus Christ.

Yes, Mama, you read right. The Lord Jesus Christ.

I know this must surely be the most difficult letter for you to understand. Please be patient and read through all I have to say.

I'm no longer enrolled at the school. I'm no longer living with the Benarmas. I'm no longer Chairman (or even a member) of the Young Pharisees Council. And, I'm no longer a restless, searching young man. I've found my peace before God our Father in heaven.

Where shall I begin?

I told you in my last letter I had an assignment in Damascus. It was almost noon on the last day of our trip when we could see the outline of the city on the horizon. Suddenly, a bright light flashed around us.

Mama, you know I have always been truthful with you and Papa. You must believe what I say now. It was as if the very sun exploded before us. I was so frightened I fell to the ground on my face. All I could think was, "Surely this is the day of judgement, the coming day of our Lord!"

A voice boomed forth, "Saul, Saul, why are you persecuting me?"

I was petrified. I said nothing for a time, but then managed to ask hoarsely, "Who . . . who are you, Lord?"

"I am Jesus", the voice replied.

So, it was true after all. All my pious self-righteous deeds filed before my eyes. I could see women and children crying as I dragged their husbands and fathers off to prison. I could see the poor body of Stephen as I screamed encouragement to those stoning him. By now the tears were streaming down my cheeks. I knew I was a dead man with nothing but Gehenna left to face.

"Oh, Lord", I cried, "What shall I do?"

This time the voice spoke not in condemnation, but rather in encouragement: "Rise up, stand on your feet. For this purpose I've appeared to you, to appoint you a minister and witness to me."

I was completely bewildered, so he said again, "Rise up and go into the city. There you will be told what to do."

When I stood up I realized I was totally blind. I must have stumbled around for my travelling companions grabbed me by the arm and escorted me into the city. All the time I kept thinking, what does this all mean? Is Jesus really the Messiah? Is he even more than the Messiah?

Three days later a stranger entered the house where I was staying. I felt his hands on my head and heard him say, "Brother Saul, the Lord Jesus who appeared to you on the road has sent me that you may regain your sight and be filled with the Holy Spirit."

Mama, how peaceful and powerful those words sounded. "Brother Saul" he called me and immediately I could see again.

He then asked me, "Do you believe that this Jesus is the risen Christ?"

"Yes", I replied.

"Do you renounce the power of the world and the flesh and the devil?"

I said, yes, I did.

Oh, Mama, my heart is broken for you and Papa. How strange these words must seem to your eyes. All I can say is the truth and assure you of my love.

Greet one another with a kiss of love. And may the joy of the Lord Jesus soon dwell in each of your hearts.

Your faithful son,
Saul

(Contributed by Stephen Bly, Fillmore, California)

LET THERE BE LIGHT

This is a good discussion experience that is also effective for a worship time together. It should be done at night (or in a room that can be darkened), and it is best with smaller groups. You will need candies and Bibles.

The group sits on the floor in a circle. Explain at the beginning that they will be doing the teaching themselves. The subject is "light". Ask them to spend a few minutes looking up passages in Scripture that deal with light. They may help each other, or they can use Bible concordances, etc. to help them find Scripture that talks about light in some way. (Take as long as you need for this.) Tell the group that they will need to memorize the passage, or at least the thought, as they may not have enough light to read.

Now turn out the light, making it as dark as possible. Give each person an un-lit candle. Have each person go around the circle and say something about darkness. This can be a definition of darkness or just a statement about what darkness reminds them about.

Next, light one candle, telling the group that they will pass the flame around the circle from candle to candle. As the flame is passed around, each person is to share what they have discovered in their research that the Bible says about light. They can quote their passage or comment on the meaning of the passage. They then light the candle of the next person, who also shares. Do this until everyone's candle is lit. You as the leader can then wrap-up any way you want. The result is usually very meaningful. (Contributed by Jerry Martin, Costa Mesa, California)

LIGHTS OF THE ROUND TABLE

This idea is to create a little extra interest in becoming part of a small discipleship or Bible Study group. The group is called "The Lights of the Round Table," playing on the idea that we are "lights" to the world. The theme is carried out by having it in the evening, and using a candle for each person to study by. You should study at a round table, and at each person's place at the table, a candle should provide the light. This way, the group is a little bit more intimate, and there are fewer distractions.

The round table top can be cut from two full size sheets of plywood. Each sheet can become half of the table. When the two sides are placed together, you've got a table that can seat 12 comfortably. If the group is larger than 12, make two tables. The table tops can be placed on top of a regular square or rectangular table. A king size sheet can be laid over the table, or you can paint the plywood. For some reason, it's a lot easier to get kids to become one of the "Lights of the Round Table" than it is to get them out for a regular Bible study. If you make it a special kind of thing, more exclusive than ordinary meetings, and ask for a specific commitment of time, kids tend to respond. Keep the meetings short enough that it doesn't infringe on study time if this is held on a week night. (Contributed by Dennis R. McDonough, Colorado Springs, Colorado)

THE LORD GIVETH, AND. . .

This is a brief simulation or illustration that involves money. Give each person in the group ten pennies, or ten of any other coin. Now take back one penny, and then another. Now the person has eight pennies left. The question that may then be asked is, "How do you feel? Do you feel like you have gained eight pennies, or lost two pennies?" This can lead into a good discussion on how we came into this world with nothing and all that we have comes from God.

To make this exercise even more interesting, you might have several items on display that are for sale. An extremely valuable item may be purchased for ten pennies but only relatively cheap

items are available for eight pennies. That makes the loss of the two pennies even more upsetting to some kids. If you use this method, however, it might be a good idea to use some play money, otherwise kids will simply use some of the money they already have in their pockets. (Contributed by Julie Von Vett, Minneapolis, Minnesota)

LOVE MESSAGE TO A LOST WORLD

Here's an idea that would be especially appropriate around Valentine's Day. Tell the kids you want them to create a love message that will give hope to a lost world; (or tell them that you want them to create a message to someone they've been wanting to tell about Jesus Christ) and do it in the form of a card (like a Valentine's card) or on a poster. Give them the option of working in pairs or alone.

Make available lots of construction paper in various colors (especially red and white), poster board, ribbon, scissors, markers, crayons, paste, aluminum foil, craft sticks, poster paint, brushes, colored chalk, etc. Also, provide Bibles and perhaps song books to help stimulate thinking.

After everyone is finished give them time to share what they have done. Then put them up in a prominent place to be shared with the church family. (As with any creative activity, only display them if the kids give their permission.)

If they feel good about the cards, suggest they make them and give them to someone they know who is not a Christian. (Contributed by L. Dean Jones, Indianapolis, Indiana)

MARRIAGE OF A YOUTH GROUP

This idea is similar to "The Funeral of a Youth Group" in *IDEAS Number 23*. However, instead of having a funeral, have a marriage ceremony between your sponsors and the youth group. Have the church decorated with candles, flowers, and the whole bit. Use scripture, poetry, special wedding music and a message pointing out the positive characteristics of a marriage relationship (commitment, companionship, team relationship, etc.). Have your male sponsors dress up in their best suits and your female sponsors dress up in their wedding gowns (if they still fit) or something white. Have the sponsors and the youth group (or the congregation if you want to involve everyone) repeat the vows with a slight change at the beginning. The sponsors say, "I a youth sponsor take thee the youth group to be my wedded partner for Jesus Christ" and then use the regular vows. The youth group says, "I the youth group take thee the youth sponsor to be my wedded partner for Jesus Christ" and then use the regular vows. Then give everyone a period of time to shake hands to confirm the commitment (sorry, no kissing). This makes a great kick-off idea. (Contributed by Doug Simpson, Minerva, Ohio)

MY HERO

A good way to seek God's guidance on new leadership for the youth would be to do the following: Have the students think about those people within the local Body of Christ whom they look up to and really respect. Then have them rank order them (first, second, third) and write down what there is about these people which they appreciate. A discussion about their Christlike character qualities could then be shared along with a Scriptural investigation about what it means to be an example as well as be a disciple. Challenge the students to also consider those who might look up to them as their examples, and what impressions they may be making. Afterwards, having prayed about the results of the survey, possible youth ministers could be approached with the fact that they have, in essence, "earned a hearing" with the church's youth. They would, no doubt, feel very honored and open to a possible new ministry. (Contributed by Mark Wesner, Ft. Wayne, Indiana)

NOAH AND THE ARK I.Q. TEST

Here's a fun little quiz that works great as a way to generate new interest in the old familiar story of Noah and the Ark. Most people assume that they know most everything about the facts of the story, but this test may prove otherwise.

1. Why did God decide to destroy all living things with the flood?
   a. Because Israel was disobedient.
   b. Because the Romans were corrupt and needed to be punished.
   c. Because everyone was wicked and evil.
   d. Because He knew it was the only way to get rid of disco-dancing and junk food.

2. Why did God pick Noah to survive the Flood?
   a. Noah was the only guy around who knew how to build an ark.
   b. Noah was the only guy around who loved God and would obey Him.
   c. Noah won the trip in a sweepstakes.
   d. Noah begged God to save himself and his family.

3. What was Noah's profession?
   a. Animal expert
   b. Boat builder
   c. Farmer
   d. Temple priest

4. How did Noah find out about the coming flood?

a. He read about it in the Bible.
b. He had a dream about it.
c. He was notified by a prophet.
d. God told him.

5. How long did Noah have to build the ark and get ready for the flood after he found out about it?
    a. 40 days
    b. One year
    c. Three years
    d. 120 years

6. What were the names of Noah's three sons?
    a. Ham, Shem, and Japheth
    b. Ham, Sam, and Jeff
    c. Ham, Turkey, on Rye
    d. Huey, Dewey, and Louie

7. How old was Noah when his three sons were born?
    a. In his twenties
    b. In his thirties
    c. About 60 years old
    d. About 500 years old

8. How big was the ark?
    a. 50 cubits high, 30 cubits wide, and 300 cubits long
    b. 300 cubits long, 30 cubits high, and 50 cubits wide
    c. 300 cubits wide, 50 cubits long, and 30 cubits high
    d. About the size of the Queen Mary

9. How long is a cubit?
    a. About the same as three schmuckos
    b. About 2.5 meters
    c. About the length of one's forearm
    d. About a yard (three feet)

10. How many doors did the ark have?
    a. One
    b. Two (One on the side, and one on top)
    c. Just the one on the captain's quarters
    d. Who knows?

11. How many floors did the ark have?
    a. One
    b. Three
    c. It was a ranch-style, split-level ark
    d. Who knows?

12. How many people did Noah take on the ark with him?
    a. Three
    b. Seven
    c. Eleven
    d. Thirteen

13. True or False: Noah took only two of each species with him on the ark?
    a. True
    b. False

14. How old was Noah when the flood came?
    a. 35
    b. 50
    c. 120
    d. 600

15. Where did the flood waters come from?
    a. A broken pipe
    b. From the sky
    c. From inside the earth
    d. Both b and c

16. How long did the flood last?
    a. A little over a year
    b. 40 days and 40 nights
    c. About three months
    d. Who knows?

17. What bird did Noah send out first to see if there was dry land?
    a. A pigeon
    b. A raven
    c. A chicken
    d. A sparrow
    e. None of the above

18. What did the dove return with the first time Noah sent it out?
    a. A pepperoni pizza
    b. Nothing
    c. An olive leaf
    d. An olive branch
    e. An olive pit

19. What did the dove return with the last time Noah sent it out?
    a. Olive Oyl
    b. A message of peace
    c. Nothing
    d. It did not return

20. Where is the story of Noah in the Bible?
    a. The book of Genesis
    b. The book of Exodus
    c. The book of Noah
    d. The book of Moses

21. After the flood was over, what did Noah do?
    a. He continued his righteous life, never sinning again.
    b. He planted a vineyard.
    c. He got drunk.
    d. He opened a boat store.
    e. Both b and c.

22. God sent a rainbow as a way of saying to Noah:
    a. "There's a pot of gold at the end of every rainbow."
    b. "Somewhere over the rainbow."
    c. "Every cloud has a silver lining."
    d. "You don't have to worry about floods anymore, Noah."
    e. "Don't forget what happened Noah. Next time it will be worse!"

23. True or False: Recent scientific expeditions have found remains of the ark on Mt. Sinai.
    a. True
    b. False
    c. Maybe

Answers:

1. c (Gen. 6:11-13)
2. b (Gen. 6:9, 7:1)
3. c (Gen. 9:20)
4. d (Gen. 6:17)
5. d (Gen. 6:3, 7:6)
6. a (Gen. 6:10)
7. d (Gen. 5:32)
8. b (Gen. 6:15)
9. c
10. a (Gen. 6:16)
11. b (Gen. 6:16)
12. b (Gen. 7:7)
13. b (Gen. 7:2, 3)
14. d (Gen. 7:6)
15. d (Gen. 7:11)
16. a (Gen. 7:11, 8:14)
17. b (Gen. 8:6-10)
18. b (Gen. 8:8, 9)
19. d (Gen. 8:12)
20. a
21. e (Gen. 9:20-21)
22. d (Gen. 9:8-16)
23. b (It was Mt. Ararat, Not Mt. Sinai)

(Adapted from an idea contributed by Charles Wiltrout, New Labanon, Ohio)

OWL ISLAND

The following simulation game can be played "just for fun," or it can be used as a discussion starter on the subject of communication, teamwork, cooperation, etc. It also can be tied in quite nicely with a devotion on the church as the Body of Christ, and the importance of each member.

To introduce the game, explain that a mad scientist has cloned a deadly bacteria. Everyone in the world has been infected with this terrible bacteria. The young people are divided into groups representing the different countries of the world. Each country is to have (1) theoretical biochemists, (2) bionic men and women, and (3) pharmacists. The theoretical biochemists are located in a top secret lab on the mysterious Owl Island. A vaccine effective against the bacteria has been synthesized at the Owl Island lab.

The task is for the theoretical biochemists to relay information about the vaccine via the bionic men and women back to the pharmacist in their respective countries. The pharmacist then reconstructs the vaccine using the information given to them by the bionics. The information they are sending is a description of the vaccine's structure (made of colored toothpicks and marshmallows).

The vaccine could look like this:

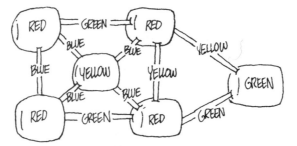

The task must be completed within a given time limit. A country "dies" if (1) the reconstructed vaccine is not exactly as the original or (2) the country is not finished before the time is up. The time limit can be made so that everyone or no one can have an opportunity to finish, depending on the leader's discretion.

Other rules:

1. Bionic men and women are used to transmit the information because Owl Island is surrounded by defenses such as booby traps, electrified fences, dangerous animals, etc. Therefore, only bionics can move between island and home country.
2. Only theoretical biochemists are allowed to view the structure, no one else. There should be some sort of screen set up so that no one else can see.
3. The pharmacists are supplied with toothpicks and marshmallows.
4. The bionics are not allowed to touch the toothpicks or the marshmallows. Only the pharmacists are allowed to touch them.

Suggestions:

1. It's best to have about 4-5 per group: 1 theoretical biochemist, 2-3 bionics, and 1 pharmacist.
2. The biochemists should relay the information a little bit at a time to relieve the confusion.
3. The distance that the bionics have to travel between the island and home country can be varied depending on how much you want to exercise the kids, and how much territory you have available. It's great for camps.
4. The difficulty of the game is determined by the complexity of the vaccine. The more complex, the more time should be alloted.

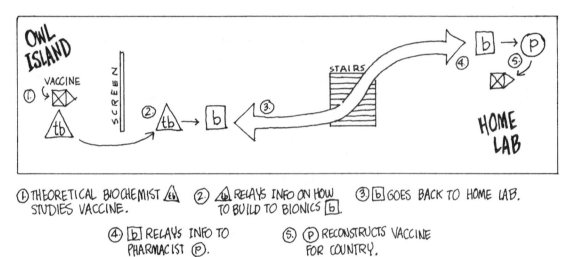

① THEORETICAL BIOCHEMIST △ ② △ RELAYS INFO ON HOW ③ b GOES BACK TO HOME LAB.
STUDIES VACCINE. TO BUILD TO BIONICS b.

④ b RELAYS INFO TO ⑤ P RECONSTRUCTS VACCINE
PHARMACIST P. FOR COUNTRY.

(Contributed by Milton Hom, Richmond, California)

PARAPHRASING THE HYMNAL

Here's a great learning strategy that everyone will enjoy. Have the kids in your group take some old familiar hymns and "paraphrase" them. They should read the hymns and try to re-state the message of the hymn in common everyday language. Do this with a number of hymns from your church's hymnbook, and then have the kids read them to the adults in your congregation at one of your services, and see if they can identify the hymn that has been paraphrased.

This exercise can accomplish three things: First, it helps kids to look for the meaning in the hymns that they sing in church. Second, it shows the value of the poetry in the song. Usually kids will discover that even though their paraphrased versions are easy to understand and conceptually correct, they still lack the impact of the original hymn. Third, the exercise is fun and gets everybody involved.

Here are sample hymn paraphrases (first verses only), written by one group of young people:

"I Need Thee Every Hour"

There's no time of day or night, Lord, when I'm self-sufficient. The calming influence of your words keeps me going. I hope you will help me, since I'm so lost without you.

"Joy to the World"

Since Jesus came in royal power, the whole earth can be glad, if we will only allow Him to be our master. To do this we must each one individually get our hearts ready for Him; but when we do this we'll rejoice just like the natural and supernatural world does.

"All Hail the Power of Jesus' Name"

Everyone, including the angels, should lie down in homage to the greatness of the Savior of the world. In fact, we should be willing to let him be our boss all the time; even our King.

(Contributed by Jerry Daniel, Westfield, New Jersey)

THE P B AND J GROPE

This is a "blind" simulation requiring that everyone have blindfolds. Announce to the kids that you're going to have a meal together, with everyone at the table blindfolded. Lead everyone to the table blindfolded so that they do not see how the table is set up. Everyone can then take a seat. The table is set up with paper plates, cups, napkins, spoons and knives at each place setting. At various places on the table, have ingredients for making peanut butter sandwiches. There can be loaves of bread, jars of creamy and crunchy peanut butter, several kinds of jelly, pitchers of something to drink, and whatever else you would like to have.

Tell the kids that they are simply to make themselves a peanut butter and jelly sandwich and eat it. They must eat the entire sandwich and drink their drink before they are allowed to take off their blindfold.

Most of the kids will have a lot of fun doing this, but some will get frustrated, some may get angry, others will try to be as helpful as possible, others will feel embarrassed and ask for help. Of course, it won't take long for them to learn how helpful their eyes are when it comes to communicating with others. (Contributed by Steve Burgener, Decatur, Illinois)

PARABLE OF THE PLANTS

This short story by Stephen Bly is loaded with discussion possibilities. Like most parables, it is most effective when you allow it to make its own point, rather than merely using it to buttress a point that you are trying to get across. Some open-ended discussion questions are provided.

One day a boy named Stu happened to be skipping by an orchard near his home and discovered six small plants all in a nice neat row. He stopped and looked at each one very carefully. How droopy they each looked.

Being a curious and determined little boy Stu marched up to the first plant and said, "Little plant, what's wrong with you?"

"What's wrong with me? Why, nothing! This is the way I'm supposed to look. Surely you can see I'm the same as the others?"

"Well, yes. . ."

"Right! That's our nature. We have a limp growing habit."

Stu frowned a bit in thought and then walked over to the second plant. "Little plant, what's wrong with you?"

"Let me tell you what's wrong! First of all, this is crummy soil. I need an acid pH soil and this is alkaline. I need a place where I can stick my roots down deep and there's hardpan here. And who can get any sunlight while that big oak tree hogs it? Whoever planted me didn't know what they were doing."

"Hmmm. . ." said Stu and strolled over to the third plant. "Little plant, what's wrong with you?"

He pointed his longest, droopiest leaf to the others. "It's their fault. I was here first. I was the first to come up. There was plenty of room for me to grow, plenty of room for just ONE plant. Then THEY came. Before you know it, we're arguing. I told them by rights the water belonged to me and they disagreed. Sure enough, the water table soon dropped, the summer heat hit us and it was too late. Now look at us. If they'd only get up and leave my property I know I could make it."

The boy politely thanked him and approached the fourth plant. "Little plant, what's wrong with you?"

But, the plant said nothing.

"Little plant, what's wrong with you? LITTLE PLANT, WHAT'S. . ." Stu stood quite still. Now he realized the plant was dead. He shook his head and walked over to the next plant. "Please, little plant, tell me what's wrong with you."

"Well, it looks tough now, but I know I can do it. If I just get a little water from over there and stretch a bit out in the sunlight and grow an angle here, I'll have it licked. I can make it on my own. I don't know about the rest of them, but I'm going to do all it takes to survive. I'll struggle, cut corners, squeeze — no doubt about it, I'll make it!"

"Good for you!" cried Stu. He hummed a snatch of a cheery little tune and then leaned down close to the last little plant. "Now, little plant, what's wrong with you?"

"Water! I need some water. But, there's no way to get it. Young man, would you be so kind as to fetch me some water and pour it around these parched roots? Then I'll firm up and be healthy and strong."

So, the little boy watered the sixth plant and it grew and grew and grew.

Suggested questions for discussion:

1. Complete this sentence: "The moral of the story is. . ."
2. Which plant in the story do you most identify with?
3. What kind of person might each plant represent? What attitudes or outlooks on life do you recognize?
4. Which plants are more "Christian?"

5. Can you think of any Scripture which might have application to this story?

(Contributed by Stephen Bly, Fillmore, California)

PARTS OF THE BODY

Here's a good way to get a discussion going on the Body of Christ and give a practical application to your own youth group. Have the kids take the youth group as the Body of Christ (See I. Cor. 12:12-27), and give each person a list with various parts of the body, along with a symbolic definition. Below is a sample list.

1. *Hand:* touches, reaches out
2. *Eye:* always on the lookout, sensitive to needs
3. *Brain:* remembers and coordinates
4. *Mouth:* knows how to communicate
5. *Ears:* receives information, a good listener
6. *Feet:* helps keep us moving
7. *Fingers:* attention to detail
8. *Stomach:* gives us spiritual food
9. *Skin:* gets a lot of exposure
10. *Shoulders:* carries a lot of weight
11. *Legs:* one who supports us

Of course, you can think of other parts of the body, with some tie-in to the ministry of the Body of Christ. As each of the kids tries to put names alongside of each part of the body on their list, they should try to match them up with members of the youth group as best they can. No one should be left out. After this is done, then have a discussion with people sharing who is listed for each part of the body. This exercise could be very impressive for kids in a youth group, but also add new meaning to the concept of the Body of Christ. (Contributed by George Warren, Oklahoma City, Oklahoma)

PERSONAL SPEECH INVENTORY

The following questionnaire can be used as a good lead-in to a discussion on the importance of what we say, how we talk, the words that we use, and so forth. Have the kids circle the response that they feel best describes themselves.

R—rarely   S—sometimes   F—frequently

R—S—F When I am angry with someone, I tell him off. (Pr. 15:1)
R—S—F I help my friends to get back at others. (Pr. 17:9)
R—S—F I respond quickly when provoked. (Pr. 29:20)
R—S—F I talk about other people. (Pr. 11:13)

R—S—F I talk a lot. (Pr. 10:19)

R—S—F I talk in ways which dishonor God. (II Tim. 2:16)

R—S—F I speak before I think. (Pr. 13:3)

R—S—F I say things that hurt others. (Eph. 4:29)

R—S—F I listen to or tell dirty jokes. (Eph. 4:29)

R—S—F I stir up trouble by the things I say. (Jas. 3:5-10)

R—S—F I tell untrue things about other people. (Lev. 19:16)

R—S—F My speech is inconsistent with my faith. (Jas. 1:26, Col. 3:8)

The statements on the survey and the corresponding Scripture verses can then be used as a basis for further discussion. Some questions that the kids should think about:

1. What does the Bible say about the described behavior?
2. What can be the result of using your speech in the way described?
3. What can a person with this problem do to overcome it?

Conclude the session with a brief interpretation of James 3:3-4. (Contributed by Stan Taylor, Clinton, Arkansas)

PLEASE ANSWER MY PRAYER

The following dialogues are great for pointing out to kids how we must sound to God when we pray. The best way to do this is to pick out various members of your youth group and have them come forward while you use one of these dialogues on them (insert their names in place of the names that are printed). It doesn't take kids too long to figure out the connection between what you are doing to them and what we often do to God when we pray, even though we don't say it out loud. God does know our hearts when we pray. Follow-up with a discussion of each situation and relate to Scripture, such as Isaiah 59:1-2, Matt. 6:33, and Matt. 21:22. Not only will this be a good learning experience, but it is a lot of fun.

1. "I know I haven't talked to you lately, but you know how it is. I've been really busy. I've had school, friends, family, and other things that are really much more important to me than you are, Marcy. But I wonder if you could help me with this homework assignment?"

2. "Hey, I know you don't know me, but could you give me $300?"

3. *The phrases in the parentheses should be said "under your breath," just loud enough to be heard.* "Can you help me out, Louis? (You've never helped me out before!) I need you to do this

125

for me. (I'm not even sure you're for real.) I think a lot of you. (When I'm not thinking of something else.) I know you can help me. (You probably can't do it.) You're the only one left to turn to. (If you don't help me, I'll find somebody else that can.) Would you wash the dishes for me tonight?"

4. "Melanie, are you John's friend? You are? Really? Ha-ha-ha, etc." (Really start laughing; you'll find the whole group will join in the laughing.) "You must be some kind of wierdo to be John's friend, ha-ha-ha, etc. I can't believe that you would really admit that you're his friend, ha-ha-ha, etc." (Then turn very seriously to John and ask:) "Will you wash my car?"

5. (To the group as you're going over to put your arm around her) "You know, Trish is really the greatest. I'd do anything for her. She asked me not to tell anybody she liked this guy, but I was sure that she didn't mean it, so I told a few (20) people. She asked me to help her with some chores, but I was sure she could find somebody else to do it. She is so nice. I'd just do anything for her." (To Trish) "Would you come clean my house for me tomorrow?"

6. "You know, Shelley, I'm really sorry I called you a Fig Newton in front of all those people. I know you don't like to be called Fig Newton, but listen, Fig Newton, I know you understand. I mean none of us is perfect, right, Fig Newton? I would never do anything to go against your wishes. Are you listening, Fig Newton? By the way, could you help me learn this new song?"

7. "Robin, I really don't need your help, but Brandie told me I should ask you. I mean, I have always been able to take care of myself. I've gotten this far by myself, why should I need your help? But this problem is a little tougher than usual. Maybe if you give me a little help, then I could do it a little better, and everybody will see how great I really am. Will you help me write my term paper?"

8. "Paul, I know you don't like me stomping on the daisies in your garden, but I really like stomping on daisies—it's my absolute favorite thing to do. I get such a high stomping on daisies that nothing else compares to it. I don't know if I could make it through a day if I didn't have some daisies to stomp on. And it really doesn't hurt anything anyway, nobody sees me doing it, I never do it when anybody else is around. I'll do anything else you ask me to do, but don't ask me to stay off your daisies. Could you feed my dog while I'm on vacation?"

9. "I really like you, Mike. You are one of my best friends, and I'm so proud that I can call you a friend. I know that if every one of

my other friends deserted me, you'd still be here. Just one thing, don't tell anybody that I like you, O.K.? Would you go to the store for me?"

(Contributed by Pam Bates, Tamuning, Guam)

PRAYER DEBATE

Here is an idea for a role play/debate that is designed to facilitate discussion on the topic of prayer. Eight young people are needed to play the various roles. They are:

1. Fred, a Christian who is struggling over the real purpose for prayer.
2. Fred's youth pastor, who wants to help Fred understand prayer.
3. A person to represent God's point of view
4. Fred's friend who is a strong Christian.
5. A person to represent Satan's point of view.
6. Fred's father, an atheist.
7. Fred's teacher, an agnostic.
8. Fred's friend who is not a Christian.

Each person attempts to present the point of view that they have been assigned in an attempt to influence Fred, who is trying to make up his mind. This can be done as a panel discussion or as a regular debate. Following the role play, have a discussion with the entire group and evaluate what happened in the role play.

For further discussion on why sometimes prayers don't appear to get answered, divide into small groups and do skits based on the following instructions. The kids should be creative and try to come up with the script, lines, the action, etc. on their own.

1. Act out James 4:2 in a family situation. The family is wealthy and has a 10 year old son.
2. Act out the parable using James 4:3 as the moral.
3. Demonstrate in a pantomime Matthew 6:5-7.
4. How would a television news team report the situation of Luke 11:5-10?

Only the group that is acting is told the key verse. The others are to discuss the implications that the skit has in terms of prayer.
(Contributed by John Davenport, Hemet, California)

PRESTIGE GAME

This is a simulation game which works well as a springboard to a discussion on self worth. To begin, ask each person to make a list of items which enable someone to gain prestige. If you have high schoolers, ask them to list items that gain prestige in school. The list could include things like good grades, nice car, good looks, being a student body officer, being a football player, being a homecoming queen, and so on. Have people share their lists and the leader selects six to ten of the most popular items to use in the next step.

Now have everyone make up a "values guide." Each participant makes a list of the selected items and assigns a dollar value to each one. The more prestigious items merit the higher dollar value. Each person does his/her own values guide and determines their own values. The relative amounts can be determined by the amount of play money you have on hand. For example, each person can be allotted $200, then the value of each item should range from $10 to $50.

The next step is to have the group mill around and distribute the money according to their guide. The group should be familiar with one another in order to do this. For example, "Joe lettered in football, so he gets $20 from me." Each person gives their money to others based on their own values guide, and each person receives money from others based on the values guide of the other people.

After the distribution, each person totals up how much money they have. Revealing the amount that each person has is optional. After the game, people can share how they felt during the game, and what it means to have prestige in the world's eyes as opposed to God's eyes. Many times we measure our world's worth by the amount of prestige that the world gives us, forgetting about how God sees us. (Contributed by Milton Hom, Richmond, California)

SCRIPTURE SKITS

Here's a short skit that is an example of a great way to interpret or to present a Scripture passage to a group. This skit is based on Romans 12:1-2, and should be memorized and rehearsed by the participants to maximize communication. You might try creating similar skits based on other familiar passages, or allow the kids in your group to write their own as part of a Bible study.

Person #1:   I beg of you, Christian youth, because God is so merciful, present your body a living sacrifice— holy and acceptable to God. This is the reasonable way to serve Him.

Person #2:   Sacrifice! Sacrifice? When I think of sacrifice I think of some pagan tribe in Africa. I see a live, wiggling body lying on a cold slab of rock. I see fire under the slab and the body burning as a sacrifice to an idol. You want me to be a sacrifice? Not me! I'm too young to die!

Person #1: Who said anything about dying? God wants you alive—a living sacrifice—which means to live for God—serving and loving Him.

Person #2: Oh. That sounds a little better. (pause) But I don't know. It sounds like I'd have to give up a lot. I mean I really enjoy living—doing the things I want to do. You know what I mean?

Person #1: Yes, I know what you mean. But being a living sacrifice means a change of mind—you no longer want to do what you want to do—instead you want to do what God wants you to do.

Person #2: Wanting to do what God wants me to do instead of wanting to do what I want to do? That sounds like a lot of double-talk. (pause) Besides I already don't really want to do what I want to do. Mostly I want to do what my friends want to do.

Person #1: Conformity?

Person #2: Huh?

Person #1: You are talking about conformity, aren't you? Your mind is set on conforming to the world's standards. Is that right?

Person #2: Yes, that's right. Uh? I mean, no, that's not right is it? I mean . . . it's what I mean, but it's not right.

Person #1: So you do know the difference?

Person #2: Of course. I *am* a Christian. I know the Bible says "Be not conformed to this world." But it's very difficult not to be. You know what I mean?

Person #1: Sure. I have the same problem.

Person #2: You do?

Person #1: All Christians do. The pull of the world is very strong. Everything and everybody encourages us to conform. That is—everybody *but* God who made us. He knows us so well that he knows conformity won't bring us happiness in our Christian life. That's why he tells us not to conform to the world but to be transformed.

Person #2: Transformed? That's a fancy word for changed, isn't it?

Person #1: Yes. God wants us to change and the only way we can change and become the living sacrifice

	He wants us to be is by putting our mind on Him. When we look at God instead of at the world our desire becomes to do the will of God.
Person #2:	And the will of God is that we become living sacrifices?
Person #1:	Say you figure things out pretty fast.
Person #2:	You know, when I think about it, it would be easier to become a dead sacrifice.
Person #1:	How do you come up with that?
Person #2:	Well, you'd only have to die one time and it would all be over. But this living sacrifice bit— it's so . . . so . . .
Person #1:	Daily?
Person #2:	You got it!
Person #1:	But it's the only sacrifice that is acceptable to God.
Person #2:	I really want to offer an acceptable sacrifice.
Person #1:	Then you'll do it?
Person #2:	Yes, I'll live for God—each day of my life. I'll become a living sacrifice—no longer conformed to the world but transformed by putting my mind on God. After all it's the only reasonable way to serve Him.
Person #1:	And the only way to prove what is the good, acceptable and perfect will of God.

(Contributed by Myra Shofner, Pensacola, Florida)

SPECIFIC SPIRITUAL SPONSORS

Many adults in the church would probably like to get involved in the youth program, but they feel that they are not really trained or equipped to do so. Here's a great way you can get lots of adults involved and a meaningful way that is easy for almost anyone.

Ask the adults in church to be a "Specific Spiritual Sponsor" of a particular youth in the youth group. To sponsor that person, they support that young person with their prayers, with birthday cards, encouragement, and any other way they feel is appropriate. In addition, they are asked to give a certain amount of money to the youth ministries budget. When an adult signs up, they can be given a card which gives them information about the person that they are sponsoring.

At the end of the school year, you could have a sponsor appreciation banquet or some kind of social event with the youth group and the sponsors together. It can be a lot of fun, and this really helps to bridge the gap between the youth and the older people in the church.

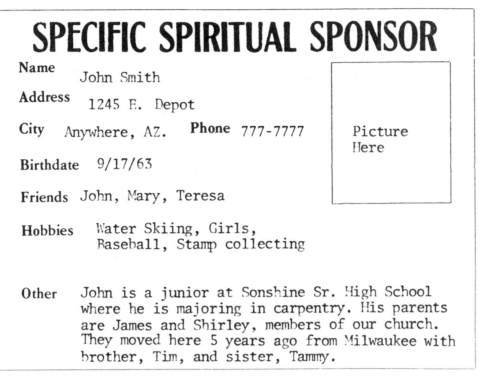

SPECIFIC SPIRITUAL SPONSOR

Name John Smith

Address 1245 E. Depot

City Anywhere, AZ.   Phone 777-7777

Picture Here

Birthdate 9/17/63

Friends John, Mary, Teresa

Hobbies Water Skiing, Girls, Baseball, Stamp collecting

Other John is a junior at Sonshine Sr. High School where he is majoring in carpentry. His parents are James and Shirley, members of our church. They moved here 5 years ago from Milwaukee with brother, Tim, and sister, Tammy.

(Contributed by Bill Abell, Tucson, Arizona)

STONE REMINDER

Following a study of John 8:1-11 concerning the woman taken in adultery, give each person in the group a small stone to take home. Discuss the sin of gossip and the warnings from Scripture about cutting down people. We often do that sort of thing only to make ourselves look good, which is basically the same reason people were so anxious to stone the woman in the Bible story. Ask the kids to take the stone home and to place it by their telephone. When they are tempted to gossip and to attack someone verbally, they might be reminded by the stone to ask themselves, "Am I without sin? Do I qualify to take this stone and throw it at this person?" Many times a visual reminder such as this can be very effective in changing behavior patterns. (Contributed by Jim Allard, Canby, Minnesota)

TALK IT OVER

This is a good discussion starter that really gets people talking to each other, and provides a good exchange of ideas on a number of topics. Divide the group into small groups of three. Each group is then given a list of statements, like those below. Each person is also given a stack of ten cards, each with a number (one through ten) on it.

To begin, one person in each group reads a statement from the list.

Each person then decides how strongly he or she agrees or disagrees with the statement. They then choose a card that best describes his or her feelings on the subject. A ten would indicate total agreement and a one would indicate total disagreement. When everyone has chosen their card, they reveal them (all at once) to each other. If the numbers shown are all within two of each other, the group doesn't need to discuss the issue. (Unless they want to.) If their numbers are more than two from each other, then they must "talk if over" and share their opinions with each other. After 30 minutes or so, come back together as a total group and share which statements generated the most discussion and which ones had the widest difference of opinion.

One slight variation of this would be to have the group use their fingers instead of using cards. On each statement, they would simply stick out the appropriate number of fingers, one through ten.

Some sample statements (think up your own):

1. I would leave a party shortly after arriving if I were not having a good time.
2. I would discuss my personal family problems with friends.
3. There are some crimes for which the death penalty should apply.
4. If I were offered a less satisfying job at 25% increase in salary, I would take it.
5. Parents should stay home from a long-awaited party to attend a sick child.
6. I could forgive and forget if my mate were unfaithful.
7. I think laundry is woman's work.
8. I think any teenager who wants birth control should be allowed to get it with no hassle.
9. I would ask a friend to stop smoking around me if the smoke bothered me.
10. A parent should immediately defend a child if the other parent were punishing him/her unfairly.
11. There should be no secrets between good friends.
12. Housework done by the female is usually taken for granted by males.
13. I think there should be sex education in schools starting in kindergarten.
14. I think there should be sex education in churches.
15. Children should be spanked for some types of misbehavior.
16. If a man enjoys housework and a woman enjoys a career, they should pursue these roles.
17. It is a parents duty to attend school functions in which their child is participating.

18. I think it is important to remember birthdays of family and friends.
19. I think it's okay for a 13-year-old to see an R rated movie.
20. Women with small children should not work unless it's a financial necessity.
21. Marijuana should be legalized.
22. Kids should not have to account for their allowance.
23. Parents should regulate how much TV a small child can watch.
24. School should eliminate the use of grades.
25. I would say something if I saw a friend littering.

(Contributed by Syd Schnaars, Delaware, Ohio)

THANK YOU NOTES TO GOD

Young people are often much better at writing their thoughts down than expressing them verbally. This written exercise would be excellent at Thanksgiving, Christmas, or any other time you want to give kids a chance to thank God for his many gifts to us.

Go to a stationary store and pick up a box of "thank-you" cards or note paper, and have the kids write out a thank you letter to God. You might want to do this following a time of meditation or Bible reading that focuses in on the generous giving nature of God. After the letters have been written, allow the kids to read them aloud if they feel comfortable doing so. (Contributed by Mark Wesner, Fort Wayne, Indiana)

TOMBSTONE TREASURE HUNT

A lot of kids are sheltered from the reality of death. Many have never been faced with death in their family and some have never even attended a funeral. The purpose of this idea is not to scare young people, but to help them realize that death is real and that all of us who are born will someday die. Here is an unusual, but effective way to get kids thinking about death for a serious discussion.

The leader should go to a cemetary in advance and make out 15-20 questions that can be answered by looking at the gravestones. For example:

1. What state is William R. Baline, PFC, 66 Quartermaster Co. from?
2. Who was "lost to memory! lost to love! who has gone to our Father's house above?"
3. How old was Diane M. Ferrell?
4. What Scripture reference is on Richard Keith's stone?

Make enough copies of the questions for everyone in your group. Take the kids to the cemetary and have them look at the stones to find the answers. (Get permission from the cemetary before doing this.) They may want to go in small groups. Some may be freaked out by the idea and just want to stay by the car. Tell them to remember where they are and to stay away from any mourners. Encourage them to do the activity, but don't push them if they are really frightened. When the kids are finished or the time is up, gather them in a clear spot in or near the cemetary for a discussion. (Cemetaries are nice quiet places for discussions.) Go over the answers to the questions just for fun, then begin a discussion about their feelings. Some starter questions are:

1. How did the game make you feel?
2. What did you think about the people whose stones you were reading?
3. What would you want written on your own tombstone?
4. What bothers you the most about death?
5. Have you ever thought about your own death?

Conclude with some remarks about death being the natural end to life here on earth, something that everyone does. We don't have to be afraid of death. John 6:47 is a good Scripture to use in building some thoughts about the Christian's triumph over death. Remind them that God loves them, and that He is preparing a place for His children. Remind them also what is promised to sinners, but resist the temptation to sell fire insurance at this point. This activity and discussion will get kids thinking about not only death, but how to make their lives count. (Contributed by Ray Houser, Fresno, California)

TURN OR BURN

This idea works well the first meeting of a new year or the last meeting of an old year. It involves the making of new year's resolutions. Kids are asked to "turn" (over a new leaf) or "burn" (an old habit). Each person is given a few sheets of paper and an envelope along with a pencil. For effect, you could print the shape of a leaf on one paper, and burn the edges of the other paper. Participants are then asked to write down on the leaf some resolutions for the new year (a good habit that you propose to begin doing). The papers are then folded and put into individual envelopes and sealed with the person's home address on the front of the envelope. The envelopes are collected and will be mailed out to these people in June to remind them of their resolution.

Next, the kids are asked to write on the "burn" paper a bad habit that they would like to discontinue. After some discussion on how one goes about ridding himself/herself of a bad habit, and after some prayer and mutual commitment to each other, each person brings their bad habit symbolically to the front and burns it in a little bonfire. You can probably build a fire inside a washtub, or use a small "hibachi."

The best way to make a program like this effective over the long haul is to plan some ways to follow up on this during the year. It can prove to be a very meaningful way to approach an old idea. (Contributed by Ed Skidmore, Arcadia, Texas)

T.V. OR NOT T.V.

The following questionnaire is designed to stimulate discussion on the subject of television, the media, and its impact on our lives. The best way to use it is to divide the group into smaller groups of three, and have each threesome fill out their questionnaire as a unit. Then come together as a total group and share conclusions and discuss.

1. How many hours a week do you watch T.V.? (average of each member of the group)

2. What one program is each member of the group most likely to watch each week? (list one for each member)

3. List three things you think have shaped your life and determined your values more than T.V. List three that have had less influence.

4. List at least five ways T.V. has changed our society, and affected our views of ourselves, others, things, and so on.

5. Rate each of the items you listed in number four as "basically good" or "basically bad" or "neutral" or "questionable."

6. In what area of your life has T.V. most affected you?

7. If there were no T.V., how would your life be different? What would you do without T.V.?

8. Can you think of any instruction given in the Bible that applies to your television viewing? Try to come up with several.

9. Could watching T.V. ever be considered a sin? When?

10. How can a person set guidelines for his own viewing? Write

three rules that you think would be generally helpful for most everyone.

(Contributed by Dan Mutschler, Chicago, Illinois)

WACKY WEDDING

Next time you want to discuss love and marriage, or related topics, divide up the boys and the girls and have them list what they would expect of their mate after marriage. Tell them to be specific. They can range from being faithful to keeping their bodies in shape. After they've done this, discuss them with the entire group, and eliminate any that would be completely unreasonable.

Next, put both group's expectations in the form of wedding vows. Write them up as a wedding ceremony and pick two names out of a hat and have a mock wedding, complete with rice and all the trimmings. During the ceremony the "bride" recites the vows the boys wrote and the "groom" recites those the girls wrote. The results are not only fun, but make a good discussion on husband and wife roles in marriage. (Contributed by Randy Wheeler, Portales, New Mexico)

WAR AND PEACE

This is a simulation game that deals with conflict, cooperation, trust, and a number of other topics as well. On top of that, it is exciting and lots of fun to play. It is similar in concept to the "Red-Black Game," which is described in *IDEAS Number Six* but involves a bit more strategy and teamwork.

The game can be played with any size group. For larger groups, divide into "continents" of eight people per continent. Each continent is then divided into four separate countries, with two people in each country. Each continent will then have its own game going. If your entire group is smaller, like 12 people, then just divide into four countries of three people per country, or whatever you need to do to get four small groups.

The object of the game is for each country to improve its economic situation (in other words, to win money) by declaring war or peace on each of the ten successive rounds in the game. To begin, pass out a game score-sheet to each country. It should have the instructions and charts printed on it as follows:

....

WAR and PEACE

Directions: The game consists of ten successive rounds. On each round, your country must declare either *war* or *peace*. You will win or lose money on each round, depending upon how the other three countries declare. This chart shows the payoffs that apply for each round:

Possible Results	Pay-off
Four Countries Declare War:	Lose $1 million each
Three Countries Declare War: One Country Declares Peace:	Win $1 million each Lose $3 million
Two Countries Declare War: Two Countries Declare Peace:	Win $2 million each Lose $2 million each
One Country Declares War: Three Countries Declare Peace:	Win $3 million Lose $1 million each
Four Countries Declare Peace:	Win $1 million each

You are to confer with your partner(s) on each round and make a joint decision as to whether you want to declare *war* or *peace*. Before rounds 2, 4, 6, 8 and 10, you are to have a summit meeting and confer with all the other countries on your continent. After conferring with the other countries, and after you have come to an agreement (if you do), you may change your mind if you so desire. That is your international privilege. You may not change your mind, however, after you have written your declaration in the column below.

Round	Strategy		You Declare:	Won	Lost	Balance	
	Time	Confer with	*(War or Peace)*	$	$	$	
1	2 Min.	Country only					
2	1 Min.	Country and Continent					
3	1 Min.	Country Only					
4	2 Min.	Country and Continent					Bonus X two
5	1 Min.	Country Only					
6	2 Min.	Country and Continent					Bonus X three
7	1 Min.	Country Only					
8	2 Min.	Country and Continent					Bonus X five
9	1 Min.	Country only					
10	2 Min.	Country and Continent					Bonus X ten

. . . .

The above rules should be self explanatory. Each country simply declares war or peace during each round, and the first chart determines how much money they win or lose. For example, on round one, if one country declares *war* and the other three declare *peace*, then the country that declared *war* would win three million dollars, and the other three countries would each lose a million dollars. Make sure everyone knows how to play the game before starting. You as the leader should act as timekeeper and announce each round, and the pay-offs. On rounds 4, 6, 8, and 10, there is a bonus pay-off which will increase the amount that each country wins or loses on that particular round. For example, on round 8, you would multiply each country's winnings or losses by five.

On each round, the countries have either one minute or two minutes (see chart) to make up their minds as to what they will declare. They then must write in their declaration in the space provided. After everyone has decided, then each country announces its declaration, and the winnings or losses are determined and written in, and the balance recorded. Everyone starts out with nothing. When countries are conferring with each other (rounds 2,4,6,8,10), they may try to mislead each other if they want to. That's up to them.

When playing, don't stress the idea of "beating" anyone—that is, trying to defeat the other countries. Stress instead that the object of the game is to improve your own country's position and to win as much money as possible. They must decide during the course of the game whether or not they want to improve themselves by clobbering the other countries, making them lose money. Usually by the fourth or fifth round, nobody trusts anybody, and each country is trying to outsmart the other. It's a lot of fun.

Follow-up with a discussion of the game, and try to apply some Scriptural principles regarding trust and cooperation, and our basic tendency to look out for ourselves more than others. Talk about reasons why we usually do what's wrong, even when we know what's best for everybody. The discussion can go in all kinds of directions. (Contributed by Alex Rollins, Sneedville, Tennessee)

WE ARE BRIDGE BUILDERS

Here's a good program idea dealing with the topic of "reconciliation," both our being reconciled to God through Jesus Christ and being called to be reconcilers ourselves.

Begin with some fun games, singing, and the like, and then divide the group into "bridge-building" teams, with six or seven kids on each team. The teams can be larger or smaller, depending on your group. Then give each team lots and lots of popsicle sticks, the more the better. They are not expensive so make sure you get enough. Also provide tape and/or quick drying glue for each team. In the center of the room place a cardboard box. Each team gets an additional smaller box which they place about four or five feet from the cardboard box in a circle (see diagram). Each team is then instructed to build a bridge from their box to the box in the middle, using the popsicle sticks, tape, and glue only. All the bridges would then be joined together (reconciled).

This activity can produce total participation, a lot of creativity, and plenty of laughs. Encourage any "extras" that kids might want to add, like toll booths, cars, and so on. You might offer a special

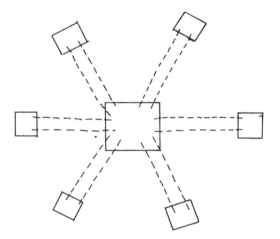

prize to any group whose bridge will support a toy truck or something like that. Follow the whole thing up with a discussion of the unexpected things that happened during the process. There will be many insights on "bridge building" that you just can't get any other way. (Contributed by Bruce MacCullough, West Chester, Pennsylvania)

WORLD COMMUNION BREAD

In many churches "World Communion Sunday" is the first Sunday in October. If your church observes this day on the church calendar, here is a good way to involve the young people in a meaningful way.

Have the kids get together on the Saturday before World Communion Sunday and bake bread of different types, symbolic of various cultures around the world. It's relatively easy to make good recipes for all kinds of bread: black bread, rye bread, whole wheat bread, middle eastern flat bread, cornbread, rice bread, and so on. You would probably only need about five different kinds. Have the kids decide which breads they'd like to make. Then have each person bring two or three ingredients with them to either the church kitchen or to some other place where there would be ample oven space.

Have the kids mix the ingredients for each dough, do the necessary kneading, and so on. Bake the loaves in a variety of loaf pans, pie pans, or no pans at all. It's easy to explain that bread doesn't always come in neat loaves. While the bread is rising, you can play some games, eat lunch, participate in some learning games, or just take it easy. While the bread bakes, the kids can plan how to present their bread for communion on Sunday morning.

Since a bread recipe usually makes a couple of loaves, you might plan to enjoy the extra loaves with the group while it is warm. Just have some butter and jam on hand. Of course you would want to save the best loaves for the communion service.

During the service on Sunday, the kids who baked the bread should bring forward their loaves and place them on the communion table. They can also explain the particular loaf of bread that they are bringing. They should tell what kind it is, what the ingredients are, where it is most common, etc. They might also say something to the effect that while there are many people around the world, symbolized by the various kinds of bread, it is Christ, remembered here in the bread and wine, who unites us all. This experience can be very meaningful for the young people as well as for the congregation. (Contributed by Sue Ann Looft, Salem, Indiana)

YARN CIRCLE

Here is a good suggestion for a meaningful communion service or a time of sharing with the youth group. The group should be seated in a circle, either on the floor or a chair. Each person is given a piece of yarn, about 18 inches long, to represent their individuality. After a time of sharing with each other in a positive sort of way, each person, one at a time, ties their string to the persons string on the side of them to form a circle. This symbolizes the unity of the group and the fact that we are one in Christ. The group may then enter into a time of reflection on

Christ, the cross, the resurrection, or participate in the Lord's Supper.

To close, the leader goes to each person and cuts a section off of the string, leaving one knot on each persons section to represent the change that has happened during the experience. The piece of string that the young person receives represents the fact that we leave the meeting as individuals, but reminds us that we belong to the Body of Christ and are connected to others in the group. (Contributed by Tracy Wiser, Frederick, Maryland)

Chapter Four

Special Events

AUTOGRAPH SCAVENGER HUNT

Here is another scavenger hunt idea that is a lot of fun to play. Divide into small groups and give each group a list similar to the one below. Each item on the list requires the signature of someone, along with a phrase that they must write out. The groups must find the specified person and talk them into writing the phrase and then signing it. The list below are only suggestions. Use your own creativity and you can make them as difficult or as easy as you wish.

Some "Easy" Suggestions:

1. A candy store employee: "How sweet it is."
2. A gas station attendant: "Fill 'er up."
3. A Burger King employee: "Have it your way."
4. A policeman: "Crime doesn't pay."
5. Someone over 65: "Whatever happened to the good old days?"

More "Difficult" Items:

1. A car salesman at a Chevrolet dealership: "Ford has a better idea."
2. A truck driver: "I hate country-western music."
3. A kid under 8 years old: "I'm a brat!"
4. A department store employee: "This place sells nothing but junk."
5. A minister: "Organ music makes me sick."

(Contributed by Dan Naramor, Florence, Montana)

AUTO-GRAPH SCAVENGER HUNT

For this scavenger hunt, you give each small group some white, letter-size sheets of paper, and a list similar to the one below. The list includes different kinds of cars and other vehicles which have wheels or tires. The idea is to get each vehicle to run over a white sheet of paper so that the imprint of the tire tread is left on the paper. Each "auto-graph" is then verified by the signature of the owner of the vehicle or by the youth sponsor who accompanies each scavenger hunt group. You may make certain vehicles worth more points if they are obviously more difficult to obtain. In addition to the suggestions below, it is a good idea to list the cars of specific people in your congregation, which means that the kids will have to go to the people's homes to try and get them to drive their car over the piece of paper. It's a lot of fun.

1. A 1957 Chevy
2. Any car with the numbers 4, 5 and 6 in the license plate number.
3. A church bus
4. A blue Ford
5. An ambulance
6. A moped
7. A 1980 Firebird
8. An orange Datsun pickup

9. A car with less than 500 miles on the speedometer
10. Any car that has just crossed over the river bridge
11. A lawnmower
12. A maid's cart at the Holiday Inn
13. A fire truck
14. Any car with a dent in the fender
15. Any car that has just driven over a banana
16. A garbage truck
17. A ten-speed bike

(Contributed by Dan Naramor, Florence, Montana)

BANANA NIGHT III

Here are some more banana games to go with those already listed for the "Banana Night" (*IDEAS Number Sixteen*) and "Banana Night II" (*IDEAS Number Nineteen*). The basic idea behind a Banana Night is to have everyone come dressed in banana colors (yellow, brown, or green) and then play all kinds of games that involve the use of bananas. Here are three more:

1. *Shoot Out At The O.K. Banana:* Get two people and stand them about ten feet apart (give them some "real" cowboy hats to wear for effect). Then give them their "irons"—which are bananas. They put them in their holsters (pockets) and on the word "draw" they pull their guns out, peel them and then eat them. The first one to completely swallow theirs is the winner.

2. *Banana Eating Contest:* Get a number of people situated around a table with their hands tied behind their backs. Then put an unpeeled banana (or two) in front of them. When you say "go" they must peel and eat their bananas without using their hands. Have some towels on hand as it gets real messy. The first to swallow their bananas is the winner. This one can also be done with couples. A couple gets an unpeeled banana, and together they must try to unpeel it without using their hands and eat the banana. It's a riot to watch.

3. *The P.B. Banfizz Race:* This is a variation of the game "Un-Banana" (*IDEAS Number One*) and involves peanut butter. Select your contestants and then cover their bananas with peanut butter (chunky is best). They will proceed on the word "go" to eat their banana and then polish it off with a glass of 7-up or Sprite. The combination usually creates a foamy mess in their mouths. The first to successfully eat their banana and drink their drink wins the race.

(Contributed by Carl Campbell, Huntington Valley, Pennsylvania)

BANANA TICKET

There are lots of games and activities in the IDEAS library that incorporate the use of bananas. If you ever do decide to put on a "Banana Night" (See *IDEAS Numbers 16 and 19*), have the kids bring a banana as a ticket. It's a great way to generate excitement and it gets things off to a good start. (Contributed by Winston Hamby, Lovington, New Mexico)

CARD PARTY

Here's a fun idea that you can use next time you would like to honor somebody in a special way on their birthday, anniversary, graduation, or whatever.

Get your group together for a "Card Party" in which you divide up into groups and create special birthday cards (or thank you cards, anniversary cards, etc.). Give each group some construction paper, a few old magazines, a pair of scissors and glue, marking pens and anything else that you have available. Each group's assignment is to make a card, using word cutouts and photos from the magazines. The words can be strung together "ramsom note" style, and may say whatever the group would like to say on the card. Nothing can be written on the card, except for the signatures of the people in the group who made the card. The "message" should be totally word combinations from the magazine. If a photo from a magazine is appropriate, it can also be included. You'll find that the groups will have a lot of fun thinking up their cards, and the person who is honored will really appreciate them and probably cherish them much more than a commercially-bought card. (Contributed by Jim Beal, Conway, Arkansas)

GET ACQUAINTED TREASURE HUNT

This treasure hunt can be done on bikes or in cars if long distances are involved. Divide into groups that can travel together. Each group is given a church directory and a card with a clue. The clues are linked to names of people in the church directory. Once the clue is figured out (the name is guessed), the group goes to that person's house and "gets acquainted" with the people who live there. Everyone in the group should introduce themselves and meet all the members of the family as well. Then, they are given a new clue by that family and they head on to the next destination after they figure out where it is. The last home can be set up for a barbeque and a time of fellowship. (Contributed by Richard D. Grobe, Rochester, New York)

GRADUATION SUNDAY POSTER

It's time-honored tradition in most churches to recognize the graduating class one Sunday in May or June of each year, but here's a way to make it a bit more meaningful to everyone. Print up a poster that features the senior pictures of each person who is graduating. It can also include information regarding each graduate's college or employment plans as well. Make sure you have it printed by a good offset printer so that the pictures turn out good. It's not that expensive.

Our Graduating Seniors – 1979

AMANDA OSWALD
Pre-Law · Miami

MICHAEL TORINO
Chemical Engineering
United States Air Force Academy

BRADLEY NORRIS
Wilmington College · Agriculture

WOODROW HARRELSON
English Theater Arts · Hanover

KIMBERLY CONNOR
Secretary

KAREN SIDEBOTTOM
Organ & Music Therapy
Maryville, Tenn.

DAVID WOLF
Broadcasting
Hocking Technical College

NANCY MADDOX
Eastern Kentucky

WAYNE ELBON
Farming

ROBERT HARVILLE
Miami University

VALERIE SHERWOOD
Hanover College

CATHY CRANMER
Education · Eastern Kentucky

Lebanon Presbyterian Church
EAST AT WARREN STREET · LEBANON OHIO 45036

Besides adding a little prestige to the whole thing (which the graduates really appreciate), it helps people to know who their graduates are a little better. The posters can be hung in people's homes as a reminder to pray for the graduates, also. Graduation really is a big deal for most kids, and things like this let them know the church is proud of them. (Contributed by Joel Baker, Lebanon, Ohio)

HOUSE-TO-HOUSE PUZZLE HUNT

This is a "treasure hunt" with a new twist that really makes it different and fun. It requires a lot of preparation, but the results are well worth the effort. Here's how it works.

First, you will need to line up a number of homes (of church members) where the people are willing to stay home the night of this event and help out. The number of homes that you need will vary, but you will probably need at least five or six. Eight or nine is ideal.

On the night of the event, you divide the group into car loads (each team traveling together), or you can do this event on bicycles or on (foot if) all the houses are within close walking distance. When the

146

groups leave the starting point, they are each given one piece to a puzzle (a children's puzzle which has eight or nine pieces to it). On the back of the puzzle piece is the name of a family in the church. They must go to that family's house, where they will be given an instruction. They must then do whatever the instruction tells them to do, and they will be given another puzzle piece. This puzzle piece will tell them where they are to go next. At the next house, they do the same thing. The group that arrives back at the starting place with all their puzzle pieces, and successfully puts their puzzle together first, is the winner.

Obviously, the number of homes must be the same as the number of puzzle pieces you have. Each team should have a different route, so that everyone isn't going to the same house at the same time. You can also give each group a different puzzle, so long as the number of pieces is the same. This will involve some advance preparation in which you assign each group a number, and when they arrive at each house they receive the puzzle piece with the appropriate number on it. You can set it up so that each group is taking the houses in a different order.

At each house there is a different instruction which the group must do before they are given their puzzle piece. The instructions can be things like:

1. Tell three jokes to the family who lives at this house.
2. Form a pyramid and sing a Christmas carol while in that position.
3. Run three laps around the house.
4. Everyone chew a wad of bubble gum and blow a bubble together at the same time.
5. Together, recite John 3:16.
6. Eat a peanut butter and jelly sandwich (provided there) and have a glass of punch.

The last piece of the puzzle for each group should instruct them to head back to the starting location. Award prizes to the winners, serve refreshments, share experiences, and have a good time of fellowship. It's a lot of fun. (Contributed by Syd Schnaars, Delaware, Ohio)

IN-FLIGHT BUS MOVIES

Here's how to show movies on your church bus next time you take a long trip with your youth group. Just set up a screen in front and a projector at the back (in the aisle). Then, just get a small gas-powered generator to provide the electricity. Some newer bigger buses have them built in, but they are easy to rent inexpensively. The generator can be mounted on top of the bus if you have a luggage rack or on the back if you rig up a little platform to hold it. It's too noisy and smelly to keep inside. This is a great way to relieve the boredom on bus trips. Kids love it. (Contributed by Dean Finley, Louisville, Kentucky)

IN-LOCK THON-A-ROCK

Here's a good event for February 29th next time it comes around. Leap Year Day is a good day to do something crazy, and one of the craziest things to do is to do something backwards, like the "Backwards Night" in *IDEAS Number Seven*.

Of course, you don't have to wait until the next leap year to have an "In-Lock Thon-A-Rock." It's a "Lock-In" and a "Rock-A-Thon" done backwards. A Lock-In is a weekend activity in which the kids bring sleeping bags, etc. and campout inside the church, and a Rock-A-Thon (see *IDEAS Number Nine*) is a fund raiser which involves rocking in rocking chairs for a long time.

To do it backwards, kids should come with their clothes on backwards, walk in backwards, say goodbye as they enter, and so on. Play some games backwards, have breakfast in the evening, sit backwards in the rockers and count the hours backwards (start with ten or so, and end with none). Think creatively on this and it can be a lot of fun. (Contributed by Steve Burgener, Decatur, Illinois)

IT'S THE PITS

This special event can be promoted as really being "the pits." Tell the group that they can come looking like "the pits" if they want, but that's up to them. Activities for "It's the Pits" can include the following:

1. *Pit Pass:* This is a game in which team members attempt to pass a Nerf Ball (or something similar) from person to person using only their armpits. Another suggestion would be to play the "Egg and Armpit Relay" from *IDEAS Number One*.
2. *Pit Stop:* Another relay game that requires each team member to stop halfway on the race course for a "pit stop." At that point they would eat or drink something before continuing on the race.
3. *Pits Skits:* Have the group divide into teams and create a short skit with the theme "It's the Pits." Give each team a sack of items which they must somehow incorporate into the skit.
4. *Human Pit:* This is a variation of the card game "Pit," which is described fully in the "Games" section of this book.
5. *Pit Food:* For refreshments, serve different kinds of pitted food, like cherries, plums, apricots, peaches, prunes, olives, and so on.

Perhaps before eating, you could have a "Pit Guessing Contest," in which kids view an assortment of pits and try to guess which fruit the pit comes from. Another idea would be to have a pit-shooting contest (squeeze the wet pit and shoot it through a hoop for accuracy). The possibilities are almost endless.

(Contributed by Joel Williams, Paradise, California)

MARSHMALLOW TOURNAMENT

Here's an event that features the lowly marshmallow. There are all kinds of things you can do with marshmallows to have fun, so why not have a whole evening of marshmallow activities, featuring such things as:

1. *Marshmallow Creations:* Give people marshmallows and toothpicks and have them create "sculptures." Judge for creativity, etc.
2. *Accuracy Throw:* Each person gets a marshmallow and tries to toss it into a basket some distance away. When you miss, you're out. Last person to stay in the game wins.
3. *Distance Throw:* See who can throw them the farthest.
4. *Marshmallow Catch:* Couples stand a certain distance apart, toss the marshmallow. If successful, they take a step backward and toss again. Last couple to remain in the game wins.
5. *Marshmallow Relay:* Team members line up about ten feet apart from each other. They toss the marshmallow down the team line from one person to the next. Drop the marshmallow, start over. Team members cannot move from their original positions.
6. *Other Games from the IDEAS Library:* Marshmallow Bagging (IDEAS Number 23), Marshmallow Pitch (23), Marshmallow Delight (22), Marshmallow Drop (14), Marshmallow War (13), Forty Inch Dash (1).
7. *Marshmallow Refreshments:* Roast 'em, or try making some "S'More's." (A "sandwich" using two graham crackers, a slice of Hershey bar, and some melted marshmallows. It's good.)

(Contributed by Samuel Hoyt, Lansing, Michigan)

MEMORIZATION TREASURE HUNT

A city park works the best for this hunt. Before the group arrives, you hide verses of Scripture around the park in various places, by taping them to objects, i.e., under a park bench, on the bottom of a swing seat, on the back of a sign, etc. Then you need to prepare riddle-type clues, giving as little information about the locations as possible. ("Something mothers spend much time on," could be a clue for under a park bench.) The group is divided into small groups of 3 or 4 and each small group is given their first clue. They are then instructed to find the Scripture, memorize it, and come back and recite it, without removing it from the object. Upon successfully doing this, they receive their next clue. Everyone should receive the same clues but in a different order. The first group reciting the last verse wins the hunt. (Contributed by Kent Bloomquist, Albuquerque, New Mexico)

MISSING PARENT HUNT

Here's a great special event that involves both the kids and their parents. First, you will need to call a meeting for the parents of your youth. Explain that you would like to help them in relating to their teenagers, and that you have an activity that will help do that, and be a lot of fun at the same time. The parents' role in this activity is to disguise themselves in a way which will keep the kids in the youth group from recognizing them. Then, you pick the busiest place you can find in your area, like a large airport, or a big shopping mall where there are lots of people. The parents station themselves somewhere in the crowd. They must be in plain view, trying to be as inconspicuous as possible, but they cannot actually hide.

Once the parents are ready, the object is to see which young person can identify the most parents. Establish a time limit according to the number of parents you have. When a kid thinks he or she has found a parent, he must obtain the parent's signature. However, the young person must give the "password" in order for the parent to sign, which is "MOMMY, MOMMY!" or "DADDY, DADDY!" depending on the sex of the parent. After the time limit is up, everyone meets together for refreshments and awards to the kids finding the most parents. You can also give awards to the parents for the "Least Located Parent," "Best (or worst) Disguise," etc. It's a lot of fun. (Contributed by Rick McPeak, Greenville, Illinois)

A MUDDING

This is the kind of event most kids dream about. Find some land, get permission to dig it up, and then wet it down sufficiently to create a big area of good sloshy mud. You want an area big enough to play games in, and preferably with mud that is a foot or two deep. Then play the games described below, or any others that you can think of. Make sure the kids wear clothes that can be ruined for good. During the event have a couple of hoses on hand to keep the mud nice and gooey, and you can use them to wash off the kids when necessary. Some suggested mud games:

1. *Mud Packing:* Divide into teams and have them cover one member of their team completely with mud (except for the head,

of course). Judge for best job.

2. *Mud Sculptures:* See which team can create the most recognizable form out of the mud. This must be done within a specified time limit.

3. *Mud Ball:* Use your imagination here. The best ballgame to play is a variation of football, with tackling in the mud, etc. Any other ballgame can also be played.

4. *Mud Jumping:* Set up a track or ramp, and have kids jump for distance into the mud. Splat.

5. *Mud Drag Races:* The guys on each team lie down on their backs and the girls grab the feet of the guys and pull them across the mud hole and back, relay-fashion. This could be done with all the girls helping out, or two girls per guy, etc. Then reverse it, with the guys pulling the girls across through the mud. They love it.

6. *Mud Slinging:* Again, use your imagination for this. You could have any number of contests that involve throwing mud (at each other, at a target, etc.). Whoever wins can be given the award as the "Politician of the Day."

Finish up by hosing everyone off (you might even take the kids to a local car wash to get cleaned up). Don't forget to take movies. (Contributed by Larry Lawrence, Jonesboro, Georgia)

NERF FESTIVAL

There are now a wide assortment of balls and toys made out of soft foam rubber, usually called "Nerf" toys. Why not collect a variety of these and have a "Nerf Festival"? Invite all of the kids to bring any Nerf toys that they have, plus you may want to go out and purchase a few of your own. There are Nerf frisbees, Nerf footballs, Nerf basketballs, Nerf baseballs, and much more. Organize different kinds of ball games, football passing contests, relays, and anything else that you can think of. There are hundreds of games that can incorporate the use of Nerf balls, and with a little creativity, you might be able to create a few new ones of your own. (Contributed by Idi Owen, Ellensburg, Washington)

ODD BALL OLYMPICS

Here is another approach to an "Olympic-type" event featuring all kinds of wild and crazy games from the *IDEAS* Library. Have the kids divide into teams (countries) and compete against each other for the "gold medal." Here are some suggested events that you can use in addition to the dozens of others that you can find in *IDEAS:*

1. *The Balloon Hurl:* This is simply shot-putting with a big balloon. Draw a circle on the floor or ground which the hurler must stay in,

and give him (or her) a balloon to shot-put for distance. This can really be unpredictable when done outside on a breezy day.

2. *Olympic Egg-Tossing:* Mark a line on the ground, and put markers on it at one or two yard intervals. Each team has two "tossers" who stand on the line two yards apart to begin with, and toss the raw egg back and forth once. They may then elect to step backwards one yard (on both sides) and toss again. If the egg breaks they lose half the distance they have gone so far. They may stop anytime they want after a successful toss, and their score is recorded.

3. *Iced-T Race:* Boys on each team wear T-shirts that are tucked in and tied around the waist with a belt or rope. A bucket of ice is dumped into the boys T-shirt (down the neck), and the boy must run around a goal and back. Several boys do this, each time carrying the same ice inside their shirts. The last boy dumps the ice back into the bucket and the team that has the most ice still in their bucket wins.

4. *Balloon Juggling:* This one is best when done indoors. Each contestant stands in the middle of a big pile of blown-up balloons. On a signal, he or she must try to get as many balloons up in the air as possible, holding them up off the ground. When the time limit is up, count how many balloons are up. Give each person three tries and take the best score. (Contributed by Lawrence Stewart, Melrose, Iowa)

SAFARI

Here's an event that can make an ordinary trip to the zoo a lot more exciting. Divide the group into teams of roughly equal numbers. It doesn't matter how many teams there are. Each team is given a list of things to do or find inside the zoo and is given a time limit to complete the list. They do not have to do each assignment in order. It is best to place point values on each item and to encourage them to accumulate the highest number of points.

At the end of the time limit, gather together at some point within the zoo (most have picnic areas that would work great) and add up the points. They must be able to display any items that were to be brought back. The winning team members should all receive a prize—maybe something from the zoo's souvenir stand.

Some sample items that might be on the Safari list:

1. Make up a song about your youth pastor, an elephant, and a monkey (50 points)
2. Bring back some animal food (15) Fifty points if it is alive.
3. Who is Sam? (10) (*The name of an animal in the zoo.*)
4. Signature of a male zoo keeper. (15)

5. Lip-prints of a female zookeeper. (50)
6. What is the youngest animal in the zoo? (5)
7. What is the oldest animal in the zoo? (5)
8. What is an Oxyrinchus Pichanosis? (15)
9. Find the "Australian Grodfog" (50) (*A lady sitting on a bench near the kangaroos, dressed strangely and wearing a fake mustache.*)
10. Find the "Great Mau-Mau" (50) (*This can be two people in the zoo tied together with string each wearing a name tag saying "mau."*)
11. Walk through the Aviary singing "Bird drops keep falling on my head." (30)
12. Pet every animal in the petting zoo. (35)
13. Bring back a dead fish. (45)
14. Sing Happy Birthday to a Hippo (20)
15. Talk to a gorilla for five minutes without stopping. (40)
16. Find the smelliest animal in the zoo. (40)

(Contributed by Tim Jack, Sun Valley, California)

SHOPPING MALL DERBY

This is another scavenger hunt variation which incorporates the use of a large shopping mall, if you have one in your area. Have all the kids in your group meet in a specified location in the mall, divide up into teams of three or four on a team, and give each team a list similar to the one below, and pencils if they need them. Give the group one hour (or so) to try and figure out the answer to each item on the list. The team that completes the most (correctly) within the time limit is the winner. If there is a fast-food restaurant in the mall, meet there for refreshments afterward, along with the awarding of prizes.

Be sure and clear this with the shopping mall management in advance, and emphasize to the kids that they must not be rude or disruptive in the various shops. No running is allowed, and if it is necessary to talk to a store clerk, they must wait in line if they have to, and be polite. Obviously, you (or someone) will need to go to the mall before the actual event to prepare the list. Make sure that you don't list things that will not be there when you have the event. Usually it is best to prepare the list no earlier than the day before.

Sample List:

1. What store is using a Hawaiian theme with leis to sell clothes?
2. What is the number on the "Think Snow" transfer at

Sunshine Shirts?

3. What is the Maximum occupancy of the Score Family Fun Center?
4. Where can you get free ear piercing with a $9.00 purchase?
5. How much is a swirl pop at Hickory Farms?
6. How many mirrors are there hanging from the ceiling at T.G.&Y?
7. What color is the courtesy gift box ribbon that has two bows on it at Walker's?
8. What are Farrell's hours on Sunday?
9. What is the address of Beth's Hallmark cards?
10. How much is a skein of macrame cord at Accents?
11. What is in a Sunshine Supreme at the Old Times Deli?
12. How much is a Realistic LAB-500 direct drive turntable at Radio Shack?
13. On the Mall directory, what number is Dr. Kenneth Clarke, Optometrist?
14. What store has a buffalo head in it?
15. About what T.V. personality is there a featured book at Books Unlimited?
16. What is the title of pop hit No. 10 at Sears?
17. How much is Teriaki Sirloin on the dinner menu at Chuck's Steak House?
18. What store has an inflatible Zeppelin hanging from the ceiling?
19. What type of merchandise is on page 1142 of the Sears Spring/Summer catalogue?
20. What are the first names of the counter attendants at Orange Julius?
21. How much is "Luster Teri" per yard at House of Fabrics?
22. What is the fee for the Easter Workshop advertized at Golden State Fabrics?
23. What is the name of the only furniture store in the Mall?
24. What store has a stained glass parrot in the window?
25. How much is "Head to Head Football" at Walker's Stationary?

(Contributed by Bob Mentze, Escondido, California)

SPONSOR PAINTING

This crazy idea is best used at the beginning of the year when introducing new youth sponsors to the group, although it could take place anytime. The youth sponsors hide and the group divides into the same number of groups as there are sponsors. On a signal, each group holds hands and as a group tries to locate one of the sponsors. Once they find one, they bring him (or her) back to a central location, where there is a supply of watercolor paint and brushes. Each group then tries to outdo the other in painting designs all over their youth sponsor's body. Obviously, this idea must be used with some discretion, as some youth sponsors may not appreciate this idea as much as the kids. For female sponsors, you might want to restrict the painting to the face, arms and legs, for obvious reasons. The purpose, of course, is to have fun, and to introduce the sponsors to the group in a creative way. (Contributed by Ruth Staal, Grand Rapids, Michigan)

SPOONS TOURNAMENT

Here's an idea which is a spinoff on the "Spoons" card game, which is described fully in *IDEAS Number 21.* Kids really enjoy playing this simple game, so why not put on a tournament to see who the real champions are?

To make the tournament a big success, send out personal invitations for the "First Annual Invitational Spoons Tournament," and offer prizes to the winners. It's so crazy that most kids will enjoy the novelty of the whole thing. Start the preliminary rounds in a large room with four or more teams of five or more kids each. Have each team eliminate people one at a time until only two are left from each team. Those two will be the team representatives in the finals. For the finals, go to a different area and have the finalists sit around the table with spotlights shining directly on the table. Also have someone in a referee shirt shuffle the cards, use new decks of cards, and think of other details that might enhance the drama of competition. Present a team trophy and also individual prizes for the top three finishers.

Something like this can be an annual event, and you can keep adding names to your trophy year after year. If promoted properly, it can be a very successful and fun evening. This concept can work, by the way, in almost any kind of games that kids enjoy playing, and which allow everyone to get involved regardless of skill or athletic ability. (Contributed by Brian Vreisman, Eagan, Minnesota)

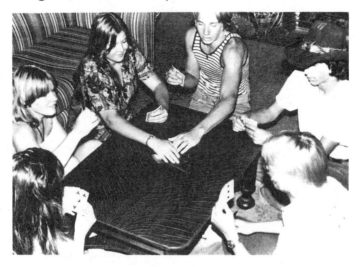

SUBMARINE RACES

This is a "treasure hunt" with an intriguing name and an unusual ending that is a lot of fun. Like other treasure hunts, you divide up into teams and follow clues from one location to the next.

At the last location, each team receives a toy model submarine (unassembled) which they must bring back to the church or meeting place and put together. The hunt is not over until the submarine is completed, with decals, etc. in their proper places. The entire team must participate in the assembly.

The submarines are easy to buy at any toy store or hobby shop for a few dollars. It is best to get them all the same. You will also need to provide model cement. After the race, serve. . .what else. . .submarine sandwiches. (Contributed by Rodney Robertson, Royal Oak, Michigan)

TURKEY EVE GOBBLEATION

Here's an event that's good for the Wednesday night before Thanksgiving (Turkey Eve), but it can be done anytime during the Thanksgiving season.

It begins with kids bringing food to be donated to needy families, delivering it, if possible, before the activities begin. Then everyone meets back at the church or another location for an evening of fun. Games can include the following:

1. *Turkey Shoot:* Draw up two large turkeys (on paper) which can be covered with a sheet of glass. The guns are those toy suction-cup dart guns that shoot twenty feet or so. The turkeys are divided up into eight sections, with each section naming a particular "action" that has to be performed. There are two

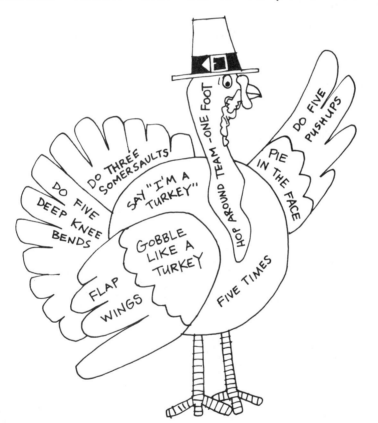

   teams, and each team has a gun. Each team elects a "turkey" who stands in front of the entire group. Team A shoots at their turkey, and whatever "action" they hit, Team B's "turkey" must do it, and vice versa. Play until everyone has had a chance to shoot. It's good for a lot of laughs. Some sample "actions" can include: gobble like a turkey, flap wings, say "I'm a turkey" five times, do five pushups, hop around the team on one foot, do five deep knee bends, get a pie in the face, etc.

2. *Turkey Gobbling Contest:* This is basically the same as the "Mooing Contest" in *IDEAS Number Fifteen.*

3. *Turkey Decorating:* See "Turkey," also in *IDEAS Number Fifteen.* Kids dress someone up as a turkey using miscellaneous items.
4. *Turkey of the Year:* Prior to the event, people can vote (by secret ballot) for a Turkey of the Year. Nominate three or four people and place their photos over a ballot box. Create a "trophy" and have a "Turkey Roast."

There are other games and activities from the IDEAS library that can also be adapted to a turkey theme. Use your own creativity. (Contributed by Robbie Sox, West Cola, South Carolina)

Chapter Five

Youth Group Leadership

HANGING POSTERS

The old cliche, "there's a right way and a wrong way to do anything," even applies to hanging posters. If you will put a piece of masking tape to the corners first then put your tape roll directly on the masking tape rather than on the poster you'll save tearing the poster when you take it down. (Contributed by Jim Bourne, Warner Robins, Georgia)

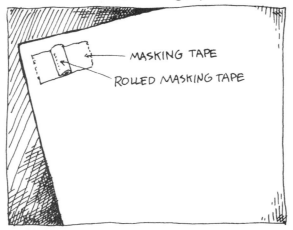

MASKING TAPE
ROLLED MASKING TAPE

IDEAS RECORD SHEET

Many times, leadership changes and memories fail to remember a particular event. Therefore, it can be helpful to record which events have been used for the next person so duplication does not take place. An "Ideas Record Sheet" will assist those who are the leaders of the group now as well as those who will follow to insure a well-rounded program and a successful transition. The Ideas Record Sheet can be posted on the wall, kept in a file, but it should be kept up every week faithfully. It should list all ideas used with the youth group (if from the IDEAS library, just the title and the Volume No.). You could also use a code of some kind to indicate how the idea went over. A possible code would be: M (marvelous), G (good), A (average), and B (bombed). (Contributed by Linda Hopper, Danwood, Washington)

MAILBOXES

Get several wooden soda crates that are partitioned off so that a soda bottle fits in each slot. Take off the back wooden panel and cover it in brightly colored paper. Replace the back and hang these wooden crates near your teen meeting room. Give everyone a slot for his or her own "mailbox" at Church. This is a convenient way to drop off flyers to your regular teens as well as a nice way for them to communicate to each other if they have a special note they want to give to someone. Everyone feels "important" because they have their own little niche. As you get more teens, get more crates and make sure new teens are given a niche as soon as possible so they get that feeling of belonging. (Contributed by Donna McElrath, Upper Marlboro, Maryland)

PLANNING SURVEY

Using a survey like the one below can be very helpful at the beginning of the school year in planning programs and activities. Of course, the items listed can be changed. Not only will you get a better idea of what the needs and likes of your kids are, but it gives them more of a feeling of participation in the planning of

TOPICS Circle 10 that most interest you.	METHODS Circle 4 that you most enjoy.	RECREATION Circle 8 that you most enjoy.	SERVICE PROJECTS Circle 6 which you most want to do.
1. Alcohol 2. Anger 3. Bible Studies 4. Competition 5. Careers 6. Colleges 7. Dating 8. Death 9. Drugs 10. Ecology 11. Faith 12. Getting Along with Brothers & Sisters 13. Getting Along with Parents 14. Getting Along with Friends 15. Getting Along with Adults 16. God's Will 17. Group Pressure 18. Hunger 19. Identity 20. Independence 21. Jealousy 22. Love 23. Marriage 24. Poverty/Affluence 25. Religion 26. Race 27. Sex 28. School 29. Suburbia 30. Women's Lib 31. World Religions 32. Values Others: 33. _____ 34. _____ 35. _____	1. Skits 2. Puppets 3. Making Banners 4. Discussion 5. Rapping 6. Panel 7. Movies 8. Film Strip 9. Role Playing 10. Speaker 11. Group Study 12. Workbooks Others: 13. _____ 14. _____ 15. _____	1. Beach 2. City Park 3. Skiing 4. Softball 5. Volleyball 6. Kickball 7. Over the Line 8. Bike Hike 9. Swimming 10. Progressive Dinner 11. Pizza Pary 12. Horseback Riding 13. Miniature Golf 14. Tubing 15. Go-carts 16. Bowling 17. Trampolines 18. Roller Skating 19. Ice Skating 20. Dance/Disco 21. Cookout 22. Hayride 23. Square Dancing 24. Canoeing Others: 25. _____ 26. _____ 27. _____	1. Fix Up Youth Room 2. Christmas Caroling 3. Trick-or-Treat for UNICEF 4. Spook House for UNICEF 5. Car Wash for World Hunger 6. Visit Nursing Home 7. Thanksgiving Baskets 8. Tour a United Fund Agency 9. Collect Aluminum Cans 10. Newspaper Drive 11. Visit Prospective Church Members 12. Cook Meal for Congregation to Raise Money for Retreats 13. Sponsor Drop-in Center for Neighborhood Youth 14. Adopt an Orphan Overseas Others: 15. _____ 16. _____ 17. _____ 18. _____

things. Simply print up the survey, pass them out and allow the kids to work on them for as long as necessary. After you get the results, you might want to go over it with all the kids as well as with your leaders to begin implementing the results. (Contributed by J. Richard Short, Matairie, Indiana)

TICKET TO A FREE LUNCH

Here's a good way to get to know the kids in your youth group better: take them out to lunch. Of course, sometimes that's easier said than done as we tend to procrastinate and never get around to it. But here's a suggestion that might make it easier for you, and get good response from the kids.

Send the kids in your youth group a "Ticket to a Free Lunch." You might mention in it how most kids today can't afford a ticket to a free lunch, so you'd like to offer them one as a gift. Basically, it is a coupon which they can redeem at any time they choose. It is good for a lunch with you. Be sure to explain that you will pick them up at school and take them to their choice of any restaurant of the fast, medium or super variety. (Not too far away.)

The ticket can include a list of restaurants—everything from MacDonalds to a nice steak house. All they have to do is set a date. You might want to make the ticket good for two people, thus allowing the kid to invite a friend. (Contributed by John R. McFarland, Encinitas, California)

ROTATING PLANNING SESSION

Most kids tend to dread boring planning sessions. Here's a great way to add a little excitement and enthusiasm for planning with large groups. Divide your entire group into small groups of four. Place tables all around the room and assign each of the tables a "brainstorm topic." (For example: "Discussion Topics," "Recreation Ideas," "Fund Raising Projects," "Service Projects," and so forth.) Each group sits at one of the tables with pencil and paper. At the sound of a buzzer or whistle, each group has just five minutes to write down as many ideas on their topic as they can. When the whistle blows again, each group moves to another table in a clockwise direction and writes ideas on the new topic.

You may want to even make a contest out of it, and challenge each group to see if they can come up with more on the particular topic than anyone else. At the conclusion of this planning game, you'll find that you have tons of ideas, and you'll also find that the boring planning session wasn't so boring after all. (Contributed by George Blakesley, West Lafayette, Indiana)

RUBBER CEMENT SOLUTION

If you have ever tried to get the last half of Rubber Cement out of the bottle with a dried brush applicator you know how sticky and difficult it is. A terrific applicator is your average underated pump oil can with elongated spout. You can neatly distribute the cement. The tip of the spout causes the last of the cement to dry sealing the rest for smooth stuff all the way to the last drop of cement. (Contributed by Jim Bourne, Warner Robins, Georgia)

Old Unimproved Method

Sticky, hard, unusable

New Improved Method

Only cement dries at the tip, keeps the rest sealed and usable to the very last drop.

YOUTH GROUP CONTRACT

If discipline is a problem in your youth group, it might be a good idea to create a "youth group contract" with the kids. At one of your meetings, announce or pass out a list of proposed rules that you have chosen in advance. (The more the better. It's good to include a few that border on the ridiculous.) Ask the kids for their suggestions as well. When the list is complete, divide the group into smaller units and have them decide which rules they want to keep and which they want to eliminate. They should keep those that they feel are fair, just, and necessary for the smooth running of the youth group.

Then have a discussion with the total group, with each smaller group sharing their conclusions along with their reasons. If you find that the kids have eliminated some useful rules or have kept some undesirable ones, you may express your feelings also. But the final decision should be left to a vote of the group. Usually they will do a very good job of selecting or modifying the rules they consider worthwhile and will be willing to honor. When all of this is completed, the rules can then be listed on a sheet of poster paper or parchment (like the Constitution) and then signed at the bottom by everyone in the group. It can be posted on the wall as a reminder that you now have a contract.

Of course, it may be necessary to add amendments as you go along, adding or dropping rules when the group agrees. Some rules may be more important than others. The idea is simply to predetermine standards for group behavior in advance so that you are never accused of being a dictator when you must administer some disciplinary action. Usually this procedure is more useful with large groups than smaller ones. (From *Junior High Ministry* by Wayne Rice, Zondervan Publishers, 1978)

Chapter Six

Fund Raisers

BAKE-IN

Here's a good money-raiser for teens who like all-night activities. The group gathers at the church at 10:00 p.m. (possibly after a ball game or other activity) to start preparations for the night. All the flour, sugar, eggs, milk, and other ingredients should already be in place for the event. These ingredients could be purchased, but it is best to get members of your church to donate items and/or check with stores and distributors about donations and purchasing broken packages or old shelf items which are still usable.

Several weeks in advance the members of the youth group should be advertising this event and circulating order blanks which list all the items you will be baking. With your orders in hand, there's nothing left to do but start in. (Hopefully, you will have several moms or others in the church who are experienced cooks to help the teens with this project.) Items which are baked during the night can be either delivered to the purchaser's door or picked up the following morning. Payment should be made on delivery or pick-up.

Teens get a great deal of satisfaction from this kind of a project as they see people enjoying the fruits of their labors, and as they benefit from added funds for the church youth program.

Here are some suggested items for the project: Apple and cherry strudel, banana nut bread, doughnuts, coffee cake, cinnamon rolls, white or wheat bread, banana bread, cupcakes, chocolate chip cookies, sugar cookies, banana cream pie, chocolate pie, etc. The project will go over great if you can keep from eating what you bake before it's sold. (Contributed by Dwight Douglas, Olathe, Kansas)

CAR WASH INCENTIVES

Car washes are very popular as a way to raise money for youth group projects. They are usually easy to organize, a lot of fun for the kids to do, and most people still need to get their cars washed. The best way to make the car wash as profitable as possible is to sell advance tickets. All of the kids in the youth group get a stack of car wash tickets to sell to people during the weeks prior to the car wash date. Most people will buy a ticket, even if they are unable to bring their car in for a wash.

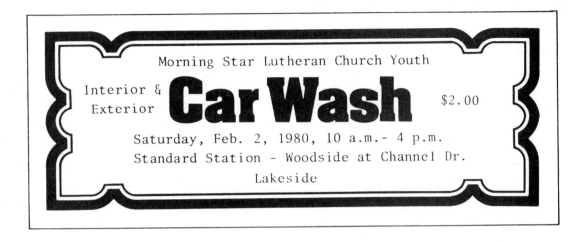

If your car wash is being used to help defray the costs of summer camp, or some other activity which requires that each kid come up with a certain amount of money, here's a good way to allocate the money fairly and provide incentive for the kids to sell tickets. With every ticket they advance sell, they receive half the ticket price off their camp registration fee. For example, if a kid sold 10 tickets at $2 each, he receives $10 off the cost of camp. So the more tickets they sell, the less it costs them personally to go to camp. This is whether they are able to help wash cars or not.

On the day of the actual car wash, the kids who are washing cars have a chance to earn the other half of the ticket price. For every ticket that is redeemed, the kids there washing cars at the time get the other half of the price divided equally between them. On car wash tickets that are sold on location (people who just drive in to get their car washed), all of that money goes to the kids for washing cars at that time. If a ticket is not redeemed, then half of that ticket price goes to overhead, transportation, or whatever. It could be put into the youth group treasury.

A system such as this insures that the kids themselves receive the benefit of the work they've put in. All money should be turned in to the youth director or treasurer, and allocated according to records that are kept. The kids should not handle the money themselves, or keep the money. Chances are they will wind up spending it before camp rolls around anyway. All money that comes in reduces the cost of camp. Obviously, this system requires some record keeping and mathematics, but it's pretty fair. (Continued by Dave Griewe, Van Nuys, California)

CAR WASH-A-THON

Here's another way to make sure that your next car wash is a big success. However, since it does involve people donating money as opposed to actually buying a car wash, it is best that this be reserved for raising funds for the needy, as opposed to raising enough money to send the youth group to Disneyland, etc.

Basically the way it works is this: In addition to selling car wash tickets, you take pledges for the number of cars washed during the day (not just how many one person washes themselves, but the group as a whole). In other words, if someone pledged 10 cents per car washed, and during the day the group washed a total of 70 cars, that would be $7.00. If each kid can get upwards of $1.00 to $2.00 in pledges, as well as their car wash tickets, that could add up to very good income for a regular old car wash.

With any car wash, make sure that plenty of kids are on hand to do the washing, and make sure that there are plenty of hoses, towels, buckets, chamois skins, scrub brushes, vacuum cleaners, and so on. Make sure each car is washed better than "automatic car washes" down the street would do it. It will make things easier when it comes time to promote the next car wash. (Contributed by Bill Rudge, Sharon, Pennsylvania)

SINGING VALENTINE

Here is a good fund raiser that works best on Valentine's Day, obviously. The youth group simply invites the congregation to "purchase" a Valentine for their "sweetheart" (secretly) on the Sunday before Valentine's Day. You can charge somewhere in the ballpark of $5.00 per valentine. Then, on Valentine's Day, the youth group arrives at the "sweetheart's" house and delivers the surprise singing valentine. The group should all be dressed in red and several members can be dressed as Cupid. The group can either write fun love songs or sing some well-known ones. After singing (which can be both romantic and silly), the sweetheart can be presented with a "Certificate of Affection" with their secret admirer's name on it. This activity can also involve delivery of flowers and/or candy (for extra cost). The elderly and shut-ins especially appreciate receiving a surprise "singing valentine." (Contributed by Ann C. Swallow, San Carlos, California)

THIRTY PIECES OF SILVER

At Easter time, an effective way to receive a special offering from your youth for a worthwhile project would be to have everyone bring a plastic sandwich bag with thirty pieces of silver in it. Any denomination of coin is acceptable, so long as it is silver. (Contributed by Jim Scott, Guthrie Center, Iowa)

Chapter Seven

Publicity

ACTION ANNOUNCEMENTS

Here's a great way to put some life into "announcement time" and to also allow the kids to be involved in a creative way. Before the meeting begins, write out all the announcements that need to be made on little slips of paper. Then, go through them and think of an unusual method of presenting the announcement that would be fitting for that particular announcement. This could be pantomime, poetry (making the announcement into a rhyme), a news report, an interview, a song, alternating words (two individuals read the announcement by each reading every other word), charades, and so on. You will also need to mark on each slip of paper the number of kids that would be required for each one.

Then, at the meeting, you ask for volunteers. You don't have to tell them what they will be doing. It might be a good idea for you to match the various methods of presenting the announcements with kids who you know will be able to pull them off. Then send all the volunteers out of the room for five minutes or so (with an adult sponsor, perhaps, to give them instructions and help) to prepare their announcement. During this time you can do something else with the rest of the group. Then call the volunteers back in and let them do their thing. You might even make a contest out of it, with the audience applauding for their favorite announcement.

Here's a sample of how an announcement slip might be written:

Pantomime — One Person

Car Wash
This Saturday at the Church
10 a.m to 4 p.m.

(Contributed by Darrel Johnson, Auburn, Washington)

BIBLE STUDY BLURB

Here's a fun way to generate a little excitement for a Bible study group. Something like this could be printed on any size sheet and mailed or passed out to the kids.

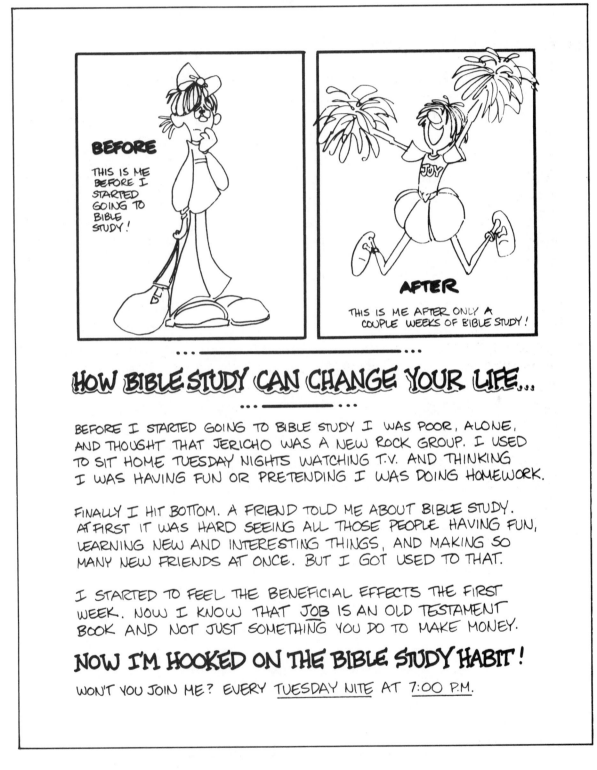

(Contributed by Tim Jack, Sun Valley, California)

BILLBOARD POSTERS

Poster-making can be a lot of fun as well as very useful. Especially if the poster you are making is billboard size. If you explain your purpose to an outdoor advertising company, they will usually be happy to give you old billboard posters free. These posters come in sheets of heavy paper about 5 by 8 feet and are great for making giant posters. Provide plenty of floor space, big paint brushes, water base paint and let your kids be as creative as they want. (Contributed by Calvin Pearson, Galveston, Texas)

BLURRED PICTURE WARNING

Print a letter like the one below (with the exception of the picture) on the church mimeograph or copy machine. Then, using a small picture on a different stencil, run each page through the machine again to put the picture in the box. Adjust the drum of the machine so that the stencil is just a fraction of an inch higher or lower, and run each page through a third time. Mail one to each person in your group. It's an eye-catcher.

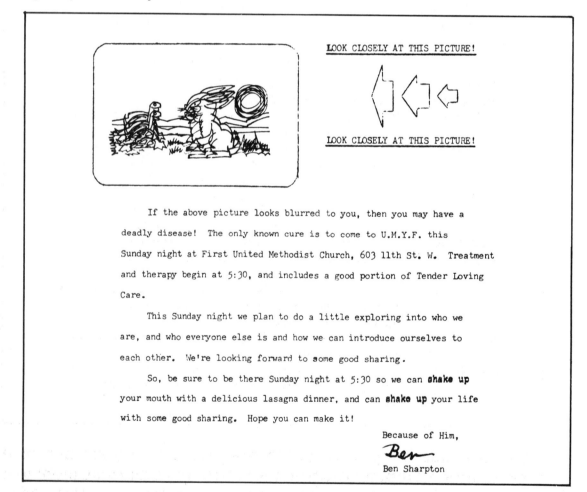

(Contributed by Ben Sharpton, Gainesville, Florida)

CHRISTIAN DATE-A-MATCH

This is a combination publicity idea/skit/crowd breaker, which can be used with good results. Send the following form out to the kids in your youth group before your next meeting. Tell them that you will have a highly sophisticated computer at the meeting which will be able to match them up with the "perfect" mate. Tell them to fill out the form and bring it to the meeting with them. The form below is a sample. Think of some questions of your own, or change it to be more "current" or to fit the kids in your group.

"CHRISTIAN DATE-A-MATCH"
PERSONAL CONFIDENTIAL TOP SECRET CLASSIFIED
APPLICATION

INSTRUCTIONS: The questions below are of a general knowledge and personal opinion nature. The CONFIDENTIAL results will be tallied by a sophisticated, high speed IBM 5000 Data Processing Computer. Answer the questions to the best of your ability, because your match will be your partner for ETERNITY! You are to use a number 2 pencil only, unless you don't have one, in which case you can use anything you want.

Don't write your name here: _____

Shoe Size: _____   Area Code:_____

Waist measurement:_____   Toothbrush: ☐ hard   ☐ med   ☐ soft

Lefty Grove's 1923 Earned Run Average: _____

DO NOT FOLD, SPINDLE, MUTILATE, OR USE TO WIPE YOUR NOSE.

QUESTION #1:   What is your name?   A) True   B) False

QUESTION #2:   Are you alive?   A) Yes   B) No   C) Undecided

QUESTION #3:   What is the meaning of the universe?   A) I agree   B) Watching Saturday morning cartoons   C) $E = mc^2$

QUESTION #4:   What is an Eldridge Cleaver?   A) Used to cut meat   B) Beaver's brother   C) Word used in poems to rhyme with Tom Seaver

QUESTION #5:   This question is an essay.   A) True   B) False

QUESTION #6:   (Multiple choice question)   A) 6x4   B) 5x2   C) False

QUESTION #7:   Do you think Christians should approve of pari-mutual betting? A) 5:2 I say no   B) 7:1 I say yes   C) I bet they shouldn't

QUESTION #8:   Short answer   A) pygmy   B) BVD   C) Fruit of the Loom

QUESTION #9:   What did the British Pound close at last Thursday?   A) 16 oz. B) 10 oz.   C) $1.61   D) stayed open all night.

QUESTION #10:   Word association. What name first pops into your head when you think of (group leader's name here)?   A) Robert Redford   B) Burt Reynolds   C) Bruce Jenner

QUESTION #11:   Did you know you are being penalized for guessing?   A) I guess I did   B) I guess I didn't

QUESTION #12:   Can you think of any reason why you should miss youth group this Thursday night?   A) No   B) Nein   C) Nyet   D) What's a youth group?

When the kids bring them to the meeting, collect them and give them to your "computer programmer." Then have him take them to a person who has been costumed as a computer, with reels, dials, bulbs, and so on. The computer takes all the sheets and one by one passes them across his "data reader" (his eyes), making funny comments and using scientific jargon to describe what he is doing. Then, as a kind of climax, the computer gets more and more excited as he reads, and he throws all the papers up in the air and yells "PRINTOUT!" The computer programmer then picks them up in pairs and calls out the names of a few "perfect couples." It's kind of crazy and kids will love it! (Contributed by Mark Shoup, Bloomington, Indiana)

CRAZY CAPERS

Here's a method for livening up your regular communication to the youth group about upcoming events, like a monthly calendar or newsletter. Just slip in a few phony events. Among the serious stuff, insert an event that is so ridiculous that it would be impossible to do, but that might fake someone out for a few seconds when they first read it. If nothing else it will cause kids to pay more attention to your communications. It can add some spark and enthusiasm to your group as they anticipate your next "crazy caper." To illustrate, here are a couple examples:

Sunday, June 31: *Over-Night Field Trip* to Iceberg, Texas. Tour of the petrified Iceberg Museum; leave church at 12 noon and return when gas is available; bring one VISA card and all the enemies you want.

Saturday, August 18.5: *Sky Diving in Hines Park* bring chute (or reinforced umbrella) and a sack lunch; meet at church (for prayer). Transportation provided by Schrader's Funeral Home and Traffic Copter #95; we're ready when you are.

(Contributed by John Elliott, Plymouth, Michigan)

ENGRAVED INVITATION

Have you ever heard someone say something like "He would need an engraved invitation before he would come. . ." Well, here's the answer. Go ahead and send him an "engraved invitation." You can print up the invitations very cheaply either on an offset or mimeograph machine. Just be sure you use the words, "Engraved Invitation" and make it look fancy. For a special touch, use the folder that photographers use to send back enlargements. You can buy these quite inexpensively. Whoever receives one of these will get the message right away. (Contributed by Jim Bourne, Douglas, Georgia)

Engraved Invitation

You Are Cordially Invited to Attend

Youth Club

This Sunday Evening at 7:00 p.m.
Senior High Room
First Christian Church

THE FLASHER

If you have an announcement to make, this is a surefire way to get it across. The announcer wraps himself up in a long coat and wears a pair of shorts underneath. For the fullest effect, the flasher should look like he's not wearing anything underneath the coat.

While music is playing, the flasher slyly approaches previously briefed "victims" in the audience stationed around the room. He quickly opens up his coat, flashing to each victim. He must be careful not to show anyone else. Each victim screams in shock as if attacked by a real flasher. Finally, the flasher goes to the front and flashes to the audience, revealing a sign underneath with the announcement. (Contributed by Milton Hom, Richmond, California)

HEZEKIAH'S PROPHECY

Here's a great way to add a sense of urgency to your next promotional mailing. Write the whole thing up as a direct prophecy or "revelation" from above. It's all in fun, of course, and the results are very effective. The following example is one that was actually used. If you use this idea, you will have to compose your own letter, using the same style. (Contributed by Russ Merritt, Dunedin, Florida)

HEED MY WORDS.

According to the apocryphal book of Hezekiah, it is said of the children of the Lord, "All those who obey commands, answer these requests, and in general serve as good boys and girls, will be blessed richly and abundantly this day and forevermore, for it is my will and my mandate that you should

---

attend these functions and involve yourselves in these things that I say.

"For the day shall come, aye, it shall be this Sunday, April 30, when the youth of First Presbyterian shall gather at 4:00 upon the field of battle known as Fisher, in the town of heathen known as Dunedin, to take up weapons of bat and ball and do mortal combat with the young adult softball team, under the dreaded leadership of the dire General Brashear (i.e., in Hebrew, Brashear is translated as "the one who grows much in the middle while losing much of the top"). Then shall the children of First Presbyterian gather upon the field of conquest, after vanquishing the dreaded enemy, for the purpose of consuming mounds of pizza at the home of the General of Light, the patriarch Merritt. For as it is written elsewhere, 'All those that consume great quantities of pizza shall be blessed in the Kingdom of Dino and La Mia and Capogna.'

"Then shall it also be said unto these children, that the day is also coming, aye, the day is Sunday, May 7, when the entire people of the First Presbyterian Youth Group, all 55 of them, shall be invited to gather at the abode of the venerable Scott Douglas, found in the land of the Philistines (editor's note: some texts translate that as "Palm Harbor") on the ancient (editor's note: some texts add "and much abused"; although this is debatable) road of Alternate 19, at 3:00 in the afternoon, for a full time of motorbike riding, refreshments, wide-open games, and a program led by the prophet Charles Scott from the far-away land of Orlando. And it shall be said that this event, on Sunday, May 7, at 3:00 at the abode of Scott Douglas, shall be for the entire afternoon, and will be filled with great fun and fellowship and growth. This is my command.

"And shall it also be written upon the walls of their rooms and the covers of their books and the tubes of their televisions," says Hezekiah, "that there shall be yet another great summer trip, a trip unlike any seen before, a trip of such astounding dimensions that none has yet experienced anything like it. For the trip shall be to the land of the holiest of holies, that mythical land called Montreat in the legendary mountains of North Carolina, at the fabulous gathering of other young foxes and studs called the 1978 Youth Conference. And the trip shall be from August 3 through August 15 during the holy season of Summer Vacation. The cost of the trip shall be minimal, with many opportunities for earning funds before the time of the trip. And all those children of the Lord wishing to make the trip should make contact with the infidel, Russ Merritt, to sell to him their souls to assure themselves of places in the rack of sacrificial lambs being carried in the church vans. Thus is my command."

Commentator's note: In this section of the manuscript of Hezekiah's apocryphal book, the author makes three pronouncements for the people gathered before his mighty throne. First, he subtly reminds them of an upcoming battle of magnificent proportions, when the worst of threats, the dreaded Young Adults, will encroach upon the Senior High territory and challenge the youth for the coveted Softball Championship. Hezekiah obviously feels confident that a large number of Youth will turn out for the battle and will defeat the uppity Young Adults.

Second, Hezekiah proclaims a great event for his people, a time of recreation and fellowship and spiritual growth, when the Youth will gather on Sunday, May 7, for a full afternoon of games and a program led by the popular speaker Charles Scott.

Third, Hezekiah intimates a heavy future program, called (we hear in later texts) "August Adventure III", following in the footsteps of the well known and highly successful trips to Virginia/Washington and West Virginia. In later chapters of Hezekiah's weird writings, information about this trip is forthcoming.

As the commentator of these strange and exotic tales, I stand by their accuracy. There is no doubt that Hezekiah knew what he was talking about, especially when he said that everyone would get something out of the events should they attend. Thus, I can only add that his words are sincere and authentic enough that I will be there for it all, and I hope you will be too.

LOOKING UP

If you have a difficult time getting your youth group to listen to announcements, here's a way to get their attention. Thumb tack or tape your announcements, or posters, to the ceiling. You can put them anywhere—in the hallways, youth room, or wherever the kids congregate. Once someone starts looking up, pretty soon the whole group will. (Contributed by Robert Garris, Windsor, Missouri)

PERSONALIZED PICTURE POSTCARDS

Here's an easy way to make personalized stationary, envelopes, postcards, or whatever. It could be a group activity, or you might want to make some for yourself during your spare time. First you get some magazines with nice photos in them. It works best with magazines that are printed on heavier paper so that the ink doesn't show through on both sides. Color pictures look best against the stark white of the paper you will be adhering them to.

Select a picture that you want to use. Use a little "artistic" judgment to pick out an interesting picture of the right size. Usually it is best to use one that is a little large, so that you can trim it down (crop it) to the size you want. Next, cut it out of the magazine with an "Exacto" knife, or a similar razor knife with a sharp, pointed blade. It's difficult to get a nice neat cut with scissors. Use a knife. Then glue it to the stationary, envelope, card, or whatever with glue (clear-drying, like "Elmers") or with spray adhesive (available in art stores). Wait for it to dry and carefully trim off the excess from around the edge of the paper (see diagram). Neatness counts!

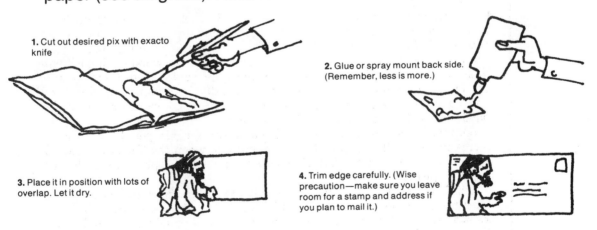

1. Cut out desired pix with exacto knife

2. Glue or spray mount back side. (Remember, less is more.)

3. Place it in position with lots of overlap. Let it dry.

4. Trim edge carefully. (Wise precaution—make sure you leave room for a stamp and address if you plan to mail it.)

Since this whole process involves the use of sharp instruments, it is not recommended for small children or even unsupervised teens. But, with a little care, patience, and thought, almost anyone can create for themselves, or for others as a gift, a stationary that is absolutely one of a kind in all the world. By the way, this is also a good way to use those "old" envelopes you have stashed away—you know, the ones with the out-of-date address on them. Just cover it with a nice picture! Try it—you just might get hooked on it. (Contributed by Brian Buniak, Linden, New Jersey)

POSTER PROJECTIONS

For a quick, inexpensive way to get the word out on an event or activity, project your "poster" on an entire wall using an overhead projector. Kids respond to media, it's cheaper than posters, and you can utilize a whole wall. If you or your youth are not exceptionally talented when it comes to art, it's a breeze to trace lettering and pictures through a clear transparency. (Contributed by Dan Pryor, Belton, Texas)

STRIKE THREE, YOU'RE OUT

Here are four absentee letters that can be sent to a person on their first, second, third, and fourth absences. It's a lighthearted way to let someone know that you are concerned about them and miss them. Print the letters on regular letter-size paper, and mail them out in the order shown here. You'll probably get a good response from them. Change the copy on each letter to best fit your own group. (Contributed by Jim Walton, Fitchburg, Massachusetts)

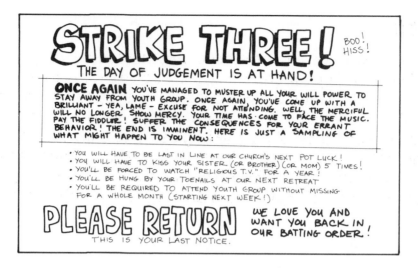

TRADEMARK LETTER

By going through magazines and catalogues, you can find lots of familiar "trademarks" that work great for composing creative letters for your youth group mailings. Just decide on your message and think creatively about how you can work as many trademarks into it as possible. Just glue them into position, write out your message, and use a copy machine or an offset printer for best results. The example shown here should give you the idea. (Contributed by Jack Jones, Tyler, Texas)

WILD PITCH

Here's a good way to advertise the beginning of your church's softball season (if your church is into such things) or any other event that you might want to advertise with a baseball theme. Cut a baseball in half (with a power saw) and then attach one side of the baseball to each side of a pane of glass, like a window. It will appear as if the ball is stuck in the glass. It should be located in a heavily-traveled area of the church where people will see it. You can also paint some "cracks" around the ball to make it look more authentic.

Under the ball you can put your announcement, sign-up list, or whatever. With a little creativity, you could use this attention-getter for all kinds of announcements: a "Spring Training" seminar, a sales "Pitch," a good way to have a "Ball," and so on. (Contributed by Mike Leamnson, Dublin, Virginia)

Chapter Eight

Camping

BOMBS AWAY

Here's a good game for junior high camps. You will need lots of balloons (get the good ones that don't break too easily) and a good wooded area with lots of trees, trails, and so on.

In advance of the game, your adult counselors hide the balloons all over the place in the woods. They should be blown up, and thumb-tacked to trees, logs, etc. They don't have to be hidden very well. There should only be two different colors of balloons, if you have two teams. If you have more than two teams, then you should have an equal number balloons of each color. The blown up balloons are "bombs." Each team should know which color they are.

When the campers are released to play the game, they are instructed that they are to try and capture the other team's bombs (unbroken), and to turn them in for points. They also try to find their own team's bombs and destroy them (pop them) before someone from another team can turn them in.

All bombs are turned in for points at a central location where the leader is. Surrounding this area is a "Demilitarized Zone," where no one may be attacked. The object is not only to capture the balloons, but to get them safely turned in. Each "bomb" (inflated) that is safely turned in is worth 50 points. For co-ed groups, you might have a rule that says that boys cannot destroy bombs that are carried by girls, but girls can destroy any bombs that they want.

If you want to get your thumbtacks back, call them "detonators" and give 5 points for each detonator turned in. That way, even if a bomb is destroyed, a person can still get 5 points for the detonator. Detonators cannot be taken from a player that already has one in his or her possession. This game is good for about 45 minutes. (Contributed by Tim Widdowson, Bradley, West Virginia)

CABIN HIDE AND SEEK

Here's an oldie with a new twist. In this version of hide-and-seek, both the hiders and the seekers must do everything by cabin groups, not individually. It's not only fun, but really helps build a sense of cabin unity, which is important at camp.

The game can be played three times. Each time, one third of the cabins are seekers, while everybody else hides. The seeking cabins can wait somewhere where they can't see (like in an auditorium), and the hiding cabins get ten minutes to hide. The important rule is that they must hide as a group. In other words, if the cabin decides to hide in a tree, then the whole cabin must get in the tree. If they hide under a building, then the whole cabin must crawl under the building and stay together.

Likewise, the seeking cabins must stick together while they search. The counselors need to reinforce this, or you can give a length of rope to each cabin that everyone must hang onto during the search. Or if you prefer, you could provide a rope (about 20 feet long) for all cabins, both those hiding and seeking, and cabin members must be able to touch the rope at all times or they are disqualified.

Set a time limit for the search, and award points as follows:

500 points for staying un-caught
600 points for catching any cabin

Each round allows a different third of the group to be the seekers. The game is best when played at night, and no flashlights are allowed. After all, it's not easy to hide a whole cabin! (Contributed by Don Crook, Auburn, Washington)

COMMITMENT LOG

If your camp has been designed for a "campfire commitment service" at the end of the week, here is a great way to dramatize each individual's choice and course of action. Stand a log about three feet tall behind a bale of hay within the campfire circle. The log should be able to stand up by itself. The top of the log should be cut at a 45 degree angle and sanded so that one can write upon the log. At the conclusion of the service invite those who wish to go and kneel on the bale of hay and sign their names with the felt-tip pen provided on the angled end of the log. Encourage each person to take some time to think and pray about the commitment they wish to make and by proper explanation try to avoid a "line up" at the hay

bale and log altar. When all have had a chance to sign their names, if they wish, insert the inscribed end of the log into the fire as an offering to God and close with prayer.

(Contributed by Barry DeShetler, Cincinnati, Ohio)

COOK GROUP CHECK LISTS

Here's a great idea for small retreats in which you have the kids cook their own food. It is usually a good idea to divide up into small cook groups, which could be cabin groups, or "family" groups, or whatever. Each group is then assigned a meal that they must prepare and serve to the rest of the camp.

To make the actual cooking, serving, and clean up go smoothly for each group, prepare in advance some "check lists" with detailed step-by-step instructions for preparing and serving each meal. It really takes the guesswork out of it for the kids, gives everyone something to do, and eliminates a lot of mistakes that can often ruin a meal. The kids will really appreciate it, and so will you. The following check-lists are only examples, of course. You should make up your own for the particular menu that you will be using.

FRIDAY DINNER
_____ Put away refrigerator foods.
_____ Put out tablecloth.
_____ Heat up soup (3 cans vegetable).
_____ Mix up ½ gallon fruit punch.
_____ Set out napkins, spoons, and bowls.
_____ Pour 7 glasses of punch.
_____ Serve soup.
_____ Clean up after eating: spoons, glasses, cooking pot, table, floors.
_____ Mix up another ½ gallon punch for Sat. lunch.

FRIDAY SNACK
_____ Heat up popcorn popper with cooking oil to line indicated.
_____ Heat up ½ stick butter if desired.
_____ Heat up water for hot chocolate or tea.
_____ Use only ½ cup popcorn per batch. Pour it in, and watch very carefully. Pour into grocery bag as soon as it stops popping (BEFORE IT BURNS).
_____ Pour butter and salt over popcorn sparingly.
_____ Use one packet of hot chocolate mix per cup. Add water and stir very well.
_____ Serve snacks, along with napkins.
_____ Clean up: cups, popcorn popper (not immersible), etc.

SATURDAY BREAKFAST
_____ Mix up pancake mix according to directions.
_____ Set out on table: stick of margarine, syrup (one bottle), knives and forks, napkins.
_____ Use 14 sausage links (2 per person). Cook in oven at 400 degrees, for 30 minutes. Drain on paper towels.

_____ Use ½ gallon milk. Pour into 7 glasses and set on table.

_____ Mix up one can orange juice; pour into 7 small cups and put on table.

_____ It would be best to keep the plates in the kitchen and serve the pancakes to the other people. In other words, take the plate with 3 pancakes to them.

_____ Your family is in charge of morning prayers. Be creative.

_____ Clean up: dishes, and cups, griddle, table, floors, etc.

SATURDAY LUNCH

_____ Heat up chili (3 or 4 cans).

_____ Put on a big pot of water to heat up a pack of hot dogs.

_____ Set out on table: hot dog buns, mustard, ketchup, as well as 7 plates, 7 knives and forks, 7 napkins.

_____ Chop finely one onion.

_____ Set out potato chips in serving bowl.

_____ Pour out 7 cups of already chilled punch; set out on table.

_____ Your group is in charge of table grace.

_____ Mix up another ½ gallon fruit punch for dinner.

_____ Clean up: plates, utensils, cooking pots, table, floors.

_____ Dessert: Set out 21 cookies (3 per person).

SATURDAY DINNER

_____ Cook hamburger for taco filling according to package directions. Add a can of tomato sauce. Drain grease before adding.

_____ Shred lettuce.

_____ Grate cheddar cheese.

_____ Get out rest of chopped onion from lunch.

_____ Chop tomatoes. (3 of them to start)

_____ Set out on table: 7 plates, 7 forks, 7 napkins, as well as taco sauce.

_____ Pour and set on table: 7 glasses of fruit punch.

_____ Warm up shells according to directions.

_____ Set out all food, including the tostado chips.

_____ Your family is in charge of table prayers.

_____ Clean up: cooking utensils, plates, forks, table, floor, etc.

_____ Mix up another ½ gallon of punch for tomorrow.

SUNDAY BREAKFAST

_____ Mix up 7 eggs and ¾ cup milk to make French toast.

_____ Use rest of sausage links (2 per person). Cook in oven at 400 degrees, for 30 minutes. Drain on paper towels.

_____ Dip bread (14 pieces to start) in egg mixture and fry on griddle.

_____ Set out on table: 7 plates, 7 forks, 7 glasses, 7 napkins. Also set out: syrup, margarine.

_____ Set out 7 glasses of milk.

_____ Mix up orange juice and pour into small glasses.

_____ Your family is in charge of morning table grace.

_____ Clean up everything: plates, cooking utensils, table floors.

(Contributed by Rhonda C. Knight, Oliver Springs, Tennessee)

COUNSELOR FASHION SHOW

Have cabin groups at camp compete to see which one can dress up their counselor in the most outrageous outfit. They can use anything that they want for clothes and accessories. The kids will really enjoy this and the results are a lot of laughs. Set a time limit for the "dress up" period, and offer a prize or "points" (if you have competition) for the funniest, ugliest, most unique, and so on. (Contributed by Shirley Raferson, Fargo, North Dakota)

GESTAPO

Here is an excellent worship experience for a camp or retreat. It works best with a cabin group or teams.

During a mealtime, a sudden commotion is caused as two Communist officers invade the dining room (preferably the Camp Director and Program Director). They play their roles to the maximum including army helmets, "goose step", guns, and so on.

The two Gestapo officers then announce that the camp has been taken over by their Communist country and all forms of church, Bibles, song books, Christian literature, and worship services are outlawed. They proceed to inform the campers that they have heard rumors that worship services were being planned for the evening and must be cancelled unless campers are willing to risk their lives by going undercover. However, if they are caught worshipping God they will be immediately captured and "killed." After it has been well established that any form of Christianity, at the camp, has been outlawed, the officers leave.

Another authority figure (Head Counselor, Camp Speaker, etc.) immediately takes over the leadership of the camp and announces that worship service must be done, but due to the invasion, plans will have to be changed. Campers are allowed one-half hour to plan a worship service. At the end of that half-hour a bell is sounded which signifies that Gestapo officers are prowling and hunting for any form of Christianity. They will be "combing the area."

Points may be awarded, first, second, third, and fourth place, according to the order in which the teams are captured. They may be awarded per minute of not being captured and also points may be awarded for creative ideas in worship, without Bibles or song books.

The Gestapo Game is loads of fun and is also a valuable tool in that campers appreciate their freedom of worship, the importance of memorized Scripture, personal sharing and music. Also, assuming good leadership from the team leader, the worship experience is very intense. For example, you might find a group of worshippers huddled together in the woods softly singing praise songs, holding hands, and quietly quoting Scripture to each other. It can be a very meaningful experience. (Contributed by Curt Jones, Lake Oswego, Oregon)

HAY IN THE NEEDLESTACK

Here's a crazy little game for a camp where there is an abundance of Pine trees. Announce that the object of the game is to find the "hay in the needlestack." You pile up a nice big stack (or stacks) of pine needles and hide one or more small cards in it somewhere that has

the word "hay" (or "Hey!") written on it. It adds to the fun when the kids don't know what the "hay" is. This would be an ideal game for a backpacking trip with a small group. (Contributed by Sonny Salsbury, La Jolla, California)

HOLY GROUND

To enhance the personal devotions of kids at camp, have them go out on the first day and select a private area off by themselves that is about one square yard. They can mark this area anyway they want (with rocks, branches, or whatever). This is to be their own little plot of "holy ground" for the entire week.

Each day the kids are given instructions for their personal devotions in the morning, and they go to their "holy ground" where God will meet them. You might want to introduce this by reading the passage from the Old Testament about Moses and the Burning Bush ("Take your shoes off, Moses, for you are on holy ground"). The kids might even want to remove their shoes each day as they have their time alone with God. At first kids might not be too impressed with this idea, but as the days pass, many kids will be spending more and more time at their "holy ground" alone with God. It can become a very special place.

To help the kids continue this when they go home, give each camper a small jar, and have them dig up some of their holy ground to take home as a reminder to spend some time alone with God every day. (Contributed by Gary Fulfer, Odessa, Texas)

THE JOURNEYS OF PAUL

Sometimes certain passages of Scripture can be made to "come alive" for young people by recreating them in a modern setting. The missionary journeys of Paul lend themselves well to this, especially if you have access to a camp or retreat facility where there is plenty of room and a body of water, like a lake.

Before the kids arrive, set everything up. Get a map of Paul's journeys and lay everything out. Put up some signs that mark the locations of appropriate towns, countries, and so forth. Existing buildings or landmarks can be made to be anything you want them to be. Use any props that you think might help. The nice thing about a camp is that you can make anything be whatever you want it to be.

When the group arrives, explain to them that they are about to go on a missionary journey with Paul. As you progress through the cities and countries, stop at each one and read or tell what Paul did there or what happened to him. You could even act some of these out if possible. If Paul walked, then you walk. If he had to travel by boat, then have the kids travel in boats. It can be a very effective way to make the Scriptures come to life. (Contributed by Aaron Bell, Greenwood, Indiana)

MEDITATION TRAIL

Here's a great devotional idea for small groups on a retreat. With some adaptation, it could be used with larger groups. It will work best in a large camp area or wilderness where there is plenty of room to spread out.

Prior to the event, a trail is set up all over the camp, with various places marked along the way as "stop points" or "meditation points." The trail should be clearly marked and should form a large circle so that it begins and ends at the same place, if possible.

Each participant is given an envelope in which they will find several slips of paper (the same number as there are "stop points" along the trail). Each piece of paper has a Bible verse and a suggestion for meditation, numbered in the order that they should be used. The kids are then sent off on the trail one by one at five minute intervals. As they come to a "stop point" they take out the appropriate meditation from the envelope and read it, spending two or three minutes meditating on the thought provided.

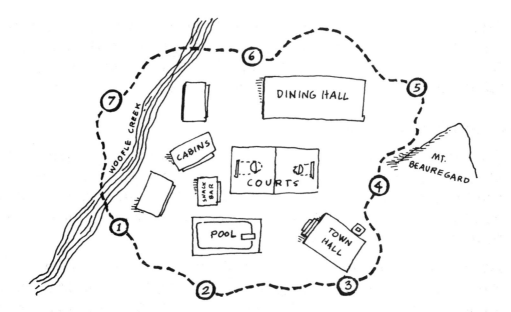

The walk should be done without talking or other unnecessary noise or activity. Of course, if everyone cooperates, there will be no other persons close enough for conversation.

If you want to send the group out all at once, then send each person to a different "stop point" for their first meditation. There will then be one person at each point to begin, and they can just move along until they have stopped at all of them. Use a whistle or buzzer to indicate each five minute interval when everyone should move on to the next point. Another variation would be to simply post a meditation at each "stop point," rather than giving each person an envelope. However you use this idea, you can be sure that kids will enjoy this new approach to devotions and Bible study at camp. (Contributed by Fr. David Baumann, Garden Grove, California)

A NIGHT IN THE CABIN

This is a good skit that you can use at camp, or it can be used as a promotional skit for your youth group before camp, just to get kids in the mood and excited about camp. The scene is in a cabin. Several campers are in sleeping bags on their bunks (use cots or tables for bunks). The lights are out and it is dark.

One at a time, each "camper" switches on a flashlight to illuminate his facial expressions and goes through the motions of writing a letter. The script (the letters below) should be recorded on tape and played back as if you were listening to the thoughts of each camper while they are writing the letters.

The last camper, Ed, should only be wearing a pair of swim or gym trunks. (He can remove his other clothes while in the sleeping bag, quietly and secretly). At the end of the letter, having just said that he is naked, he gets up and starts to walk across the room. At an agreed upon point, all the other campers switch on their lights and train them on Ed, who doubles over in embarrassment and runs out screaming.

Fill in the blanks in the funniest way possible. You might want to have your adult sponsors or counselors play the parts for added fun.

The Letters (you can create your own to fit your own camp):

Dear Mom,

Here I am at _____. Everyone is asleep now, so I
　　　　　　　　　　(camp name)
thought I would write you a note! _____ is snoring. I
　　　　　　　　　　　　　　　　　　　(girl in group)
had a great time today! I especially enjoyed the singing and our small

groups. In our small groups we talked about our lives and hopes. I know

_____, _____, and _____ so much better now.
　(guy)　　　　　　　(girl)　　　　　　　　(guy)
Well, I have to get to sleep, we have so much to do tomorrow!

　　　　　　　　　　　　　　　　　　　　　　Love,　Molly

Dear Susan,

I thought about you a lot today. We did some thinking and sharing about

the importance of relationships. I thought of you because you have been

such an important person to me. Thank you for listening to me, and ac-

cepting my honest feelings.

We are having some great talks here. _____ has a
　　　　　　　　　　　　　　　　　　　　　　　　　(youth minister)
few good ideas! Today we spent some time thinking about the future. I am

so excited about what God will be doing in my life. Well, better go now, see

you at school.

Dear Journal,

The first day at camp has been very exciting. I didn't realize there would

be so many cute boys here!!!

This morning I ate breakfast with _____. That hunk,
　　　　　　　　　　　　　　　　　　　(sophomore guy)
_____ is in my small group. I sat by _____ in the morn-
　(junior guy)　　　　　　　　　　　　　　　　(senior guy)
ing meeting and _____ flirted with me all day. But of course he
　　　　　　　　　　(biggest flirt)
flirts with everyone. _____ and I went for a walk this afternoon.
　　　　　　　　　　　(junior guy)
_____ saved a place for me at dinner.
　(senior guy)
Then, (sigh) in the evening, I talked for hours with _____.
　　　　　　　　　　　　　　　　　　　　　　　　　　　(most desireable guy)
Everyone was so jealous. I don't know why! If they only knew my heart be-

---

188

longs to _____. (Sigh). But he doesn't even know I exist. Oh well,
(most shy guy)
maybe tomorrow.

Jack,

Too bad you missed this retreat! It is a blast. You should see all the snow
around here. I smeared _____ so bad. He's still moan-
(freshman guy)
ing. Our cabin challenged everyone else to a snow war. We held them off at
first—then we got wiped out! After that we smashed _____.
(three girls)
The inner tubes were the greatest. We slid down the mountain almost all
afternoon! You should see this guy they call _____!!
(a riotous counselor)
He's a wild man.

I've learned a lot about Christ too!! I have a lot to tell you about that!!
P.S. We hid all of Ed's clothes so he had to run from the shower in his towel.
Now he's in his sleeping bag naked.

Bob

Dear Grover,

What a day! I've never learned so much about my life!!! I feel like God
has really spoken to me here! I never knew He loved me so much. I also
didn't know what a great responsibility it is to be a Christian. I really have a
direction to move now!

This is a great place, plenty of fun and lots of good food as well!! The kids
are great. Even though some of the guys have taken all my clothes and I am
in my sleeping bag naked.

I think I'll go look for my clothes now, while everyone's asleep!

Yours truly,   Ed

(Contributed by Rex McDaniel, Tustin, California)

REVOLVING DOOR CAMP

Many times when you plan a camp, you discover that some people
can't come for the entire week because of jobs or finances, but they
would like to come for a day or two, or some other part of it. Usually
that only creates problems, since you like to have some continuity
with most camp programs, and it's hard when people come and go.

But what if you just planned a camp with that in mind? This would
especially be appropriate with older youth, like college students,
who are usually broke, have summer jobs, and so forth. Plan a camp
in which kids can come whenever they can. Hold it somewhere that

is close, charge them by the meal, by the day (or night), and plan programs and activities that can be done by any number, and aren't presented in a series of some kind.

One group did this by reserving a group camping area at a local beach during the summer. A main supply tent was set up with food and a place for kids to change clothes, and those who came just brought a sleeping bag and "slept out." Everybody cooked their own food on open fires or camp stoves, and the overall response was better than any other camp the group had ever done. One or two adult couples remained there the entire week, but they were the only "live-in" campers. Everyone else came when they could. Use your own creativity and this type of camp can be a real success for your group, too. (Contributed by Wilber Griffith, El Segundo, California)

SECRET PALS

This is a good community-building exercise for your next camp or retreat. At the beginning of the week or weekend, have everyone write their names on little slips of paper. Place all the names in a box, and have everyone draw a name (not their own). This name is to be their "secret pal" throughout the camp or retreat. They are instructed to perform small acts of friendship for their secret pal, but always doing it in secret, so that they won't know who is responsible. For example, a person might send their secret pal a bouquet of flowers, a love letter, a box of candy, or arrange for them not to have to do "K.P."

At the end of the experience, the veil of secrecy can be removed, and usually the results are very good. Some lasting friendships can get started this way. (Contributed by Gail Moody, Newtown, Pennsylvania)

SOFT SHOE

Here's a game for camps in a wooded area where you have lots of leaves and twigs on the ground. Have the group form a circle about twenty feet or so in diameter. One person is chosen to be it and stands in the center of the circle with a blindfold on. The group in the circle must be absolutely quiet. One person at a time is chosen to try and sneak up on "it" by walking over the leaves and twigs without making any noise. If the blindfolded person hears the approaching person before being tagged, "it" points in the direction of the noise and yells out "soft shoe!" The person who is discovered must then return to the circle and try again, or another person is chosen. (Contributed by Butch Garman, Knoxville, Tennessee)

SURPRISE PACKAGES FROM HOME

Most kids love to get something in the mail when they are away at camp. It can be quite disappointing for kids when they hope they will get something, but nothing ever comes. To remedy this, secretly contact all the parents of the campers in advance, and ask them to prepare a "surprise package" for their child. These can be collected without the kids knowing anything about them, and then, on whichever day you choose, they can all be handed out at once. The kids will freak out. You might want to specify to the parents the type of thing that would be best in the package, but let each parent give whatever they want. It would also be a good idea to take a few "extras," just in case.

A good variation of this, with perhaps a lot more meaning, would be to have a session at camp on "self-worth," or on talents, gifts, abilities, and the like. During the session, kids can get into small groups, and do a type of self-evaluation, asking themselves questions like "What are my strengths? What are my abilities and how can I best use them?" Then, toward the conclusion of this session, surprise packages can be produced from each camper's parents, with a note from the parents affirming the strengths and special abilities in their child. The gift in the package can be symbolic of the gifts that the child brings to the family. Again, these surprise packages should be collected and stashed away without the kids knowing anything about them. The kids can then share these gifts with each other if they want. The results of something like this can be very effective. (Contributed by Dennis McDonough, Colorado Springs, Colorado)

UP BOARD

Camps and retreats are usually "up" experiences for a youth group. So why not benefit from them all year round? Have the group create an "UP BOARD" which is nothing more than a bulletin board that is reserved for photos and other mementos from past camps, retreats, or other "mountaintop" highs that the group has had. Whenever someone is feeling a little "down" they should get a real lift from looking at the "Up Board." (Contributed by Donna McElrath, Upper Marlboro, Maryland)

WILDERNESS WORSHIP CENTER

Many retreats will conclude with a worship service on Sunday morning. A great way for a group to create their own place for this worship service is to find an open area around the camp somewhere that is surrounded by trees, or posts. Take a roll of good strong rope, or cord or wire and wrap it around the area about four or five feet above the ground. It doesn't have to be a perfect square.

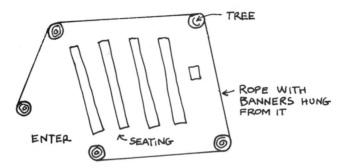

On the day before the worship service, have all the campers make banners or posters on a common theme, or on anything they want. Then, prior to the worship service, have the kids hang their banners and posters on the line around the worship area. Depending on the location, you can provide chairs or logs for seating or the kids can sit on the ground. The worship will have added meaning since the kids have actually created their own church for the service. (Contributed by Chuck Campbell, Port Clinton, Ohio)

WOODSMAN'S FROLIC

By using all natural objects at a campsite or retreat area, you can plan an entire afternoon of games which might have been played at one time by a lumberjack or back woodsman. It should be set up with a carnival-type atmosphere and it can be used with all ages. You might want to call it "Paul Bunyan Day" or something like that. Here are some possible events:

1. *Ring Toss:* In the woods there are usually many types of vines. You can fashion them into rings (circles), tied together with twine. Put some stakes in the ground, mark off a throwing line, and award points depending on the difficulty of the toss. If you don't have vines, use rope, wire, or whatever you have.
2. *Log Walk:* Cut a log that is about two feet in diameter, and as close to being circular as possible. It is placed at a starting line, and kids try to balance on it and "walk it" to the finish line. If they fall off, they must start over.
3. *Log Rolling:* Use the same log as above. Have two people get on each end and have an old time contest of trying to roll the other off.
4. *Log Pulling:* Cut a log and notch it so that a rope can be tied around it. Kids then compete to pull it a certain distance for the best time. You might have different sizes of logs for different age groups. Individuals can compete or teams (pulling on the rope like a tug-o-war).

5. *Log Sawing/Chopping:* Get an axe or a big lumberjack hand saw and have teams race to see who can cut a log in half in the fastest time. For teams, each person in line would take two swings with the axe or saw two times across, then go to the end of the line.

6. *Log Bowling:* Choose a sturdy branch on a tree and tie a rope to it. Then tie on a log (hanging straight down). Stand four slender logs on end around the hanging log. The hanging log then becomes the "bowling ball," and it is pulled back about twenty feet, and released to try and knock down the pins.

7. *Log Throw:* This is sort of like a javelin throw. Get a long, slender log, and have the kids throw it for distance.

(Contributed by Butch Garman, Knoxville, Tennessee)

Chapter Nine

Family Ministry

FAMILIES ALIVE

The purpose of this game is to symbolically demonstrate the joy of family cooperation in presenting the Gospel to the world, and the necessity of other families to share the ministry.

A burning flare will represent the time remaining before the world ends. When the flares are out the game is over and the world has ended. The game is not a race but a cooperative adventure.

Set up the ten stations with the flare and *Living Spring* in a large open area that is easily visible. Each station should be 20 to 50 feet apart. This will give a sense of accomplishment and prevent crowding. Each station should be identified to prevent confusion. Families should check off stations as they complete them.

There are ten symbolic activities. *Restoring Human Dignity* must be done first, and *Living Spring* done last. All others can be done at random when the station is vacant. To begin the game, just light a flare. As long as the flare is lit, the game proceeds. Have several flares on hand and light one before the other goes out.

The final station is the *Living Spring*. Have clean water in the container. The second bucket is placed 10 feet away from the spring. Paper cups and a ladle should be easily accessible. Water placed into the second bucket is used to extinguish the flare when all families have completed the 10 stations. It is best if the flares are extinguished. However, if the flares are used up before the game is completed, just end the game as if the world's time ran out. Even though the world "ended," families can still rejoice in what they have accomplished. Follow the game with a time of discussion.

Supplies needed:

String and balloons for everyone, scissors
Crackers (1 box)
Cloth for 5 blindfolds
Empty milk cartons (at least 20)
Scrap paper or newspaper and a trash can (separated by 10 feet)
Bandaids or tape (scissors)
Large coat and hat
Bible (2 or 3 if you have a large group)

Three flares, matches
Paper cups (one for each family unit)
Two large water containers, one with clean water (use ladle to fill each family's cup).

Activities (this list should be printed up for each family):

_____ 1. *Restore Human Dignity*: Tie a balloon on each other's waist. (Human Dignity must be maintained throughout the game.) If a balloon breaks you must all go back to the Human Dignity Station to obtain another.

_____ 2. *Feed the Hungry*: Feed each other crackers.

_____ 3. *Free the Captives*: Blindfold all members but one, for he will lead you to the next station. Remove the blindfolds and return them to the statio *before* doing the next activity.

_____ 4. *Rebuild the Nations*: Build a tower by stacking the empty milk cartons. They must remain stacked for 15 seconds.

_____ 5. *Clean up the Environment*: Line up in a straight line. Take a sheet of paper, crumble it up and pass it down the line to the last person who drops it into the trash can.

_____ 6. *Heal the Sick*: Put a "bandaid" on each other. Each person does all the others in the family, so you will have tape from all members. Leave the tape on until the game is over.

_____ 7. *Clothe the Naked*: Put on a coat and hat and give it to the next member until all have had a turn.

_____ 8. *Welcome Strangers*: Stop another family and greet each of their members, shaking hands and inviting them to visit you again.

_____ 9. *Preach the Word*: Select a family member to read aloud Matthew 25:31-46.

_____10. *Living Spring*: After you have completed all of the above activities, take *a* cup and fill it full of water from the Living Spring and each member take a sip of water from it. Refill the cup and pour it into the second water container. Wait nearby once you have finished.

(Contributed by Gary Ogdon, Minneapolis, Minnesota)

FAMILY NEWLYWED GAME

Here's a family version of TV's "Newlywed Game" that is very effective as a way for families to communicate with each other in a lighthearted manner. Print up the questions below, one set for the youth, and one set for the parents; have them write out their answers. Then have each family comes forward one at a time to try and earn as many points as possible by guessing each other's answers.

The parents should complete one sheet of answers (rather than two) and likewise for the kids if there is more than one child. (They should agree on some common answers.) When the family comes forward, the questions can go back and forth. You ask the first "parent question," and the youth tries to guess how their parents answered. After the parents reveal their answer (and the points are awarded if the guess is correct), the first "youth question" is asked, and the parents guess. This goes back and forth until all the questions have been asked. Following the game (after all the families have played), you might have each family meet together for five or ten minutes and discuss their answers with each other.

The following questions are only suggestions, but they give you the idea. Use fewer questions if you have a lot of families and not much time; more questions if you have plenty of time.

Questions for the youth:

1. Name something you do that really annoys your parents.
2. What would you like to be when you are your parents' age?
3. What is the neatest thing your family has done this year?
4. What is your favorite time of the day?
5. How are you most like your parents?
6. What is a tell-tale sign that your parents are in a bad mood?
7. What is one of the nicest things your parents have done for you recently?
8. Name something you wish your family would do together some day?

Questions for the parents:

1. At 17, what did you want to be as an adult?
2. What do you value most around your house?
3. What one thing makes you most proud of your children?
4. When was the last time you and your family had a good laugh together?
5. How do you know when your kids are upset about something?
6. How old think your son/daughter should be when they move out of the house?

7. What do you enjoy doing in your spare time?
8. What is the best gift you have given your son/daughter in the past year?

(Contributed by James D. Stender, Indianapolis, Indiana)

FAMILY VOLLEYBALL

Here's a good version of volleyball that works great when families are together. Make sure everyone is in a family group. If someone is present who is not with his or her family, then find a family that they can be a part of for this game.

Basically the game is regular volleyball, but each family sends one family member at a time into the game to play for their family. If you have a total of 20 families, then there would be 10 people on each side of the net, one from each family. Each family has the freedom to rotate their family members in and out of the game as they please, or this aspect of it could be organized in some way. The important thing is that the rest of the families (those not in the game) should cheer on their family members who are playing, and the team their family is on. This should be spelled out as a requirement of the game—lots of yelling and rooting for your family's player. The results of kids yelling for their parents and parents yelling for their kids are fantastic. It really creates a positive affirming experience for everyone. (Contributed by Waymon Hinson, Memphis, Tennessee)

LETTER EXCHANGE

This idea can be used in conjunction with any program that involves teenagers and their parents. Each young person is asked to think through and to compose a letter than can be presented to his/her parents, and vice versa. If this is done in the proper atmosphere, the results can be very good. It should not be done frivolously, or without adequate preparation. How you set this up, and what you ask people to include in the letters is pretty much left up to you. Below are some sample letter suggestions to be given to the youth and to the parents.

For Teenagers:

If your parents were to die suddenly, there are things you would want them to have known, things you carry in your heart and don't ordinarily speak, things they need to know.

As you and they reach the end of your childhood, it becomes possible for you to see clearly what they have given you over the years, and it becomes possible for you to put into words the love and gratitude you feel.

Let this letter be an occasion to tell them what you've received from them and what they mean to you. Let it be an occasion to share with them the beginnings of faith which their faithfulness to you has made possible. Let this be the letter when you put into words both your love for them and the faith you will take with you as you go out from under their care

197

and into the world.

And lastly, if there are some changes you'd like to make in your day-to-day life with them, some new gift of yourself, that will make your final years in their home more meaningful, you could include that also in your letter.

Enjoy the writing. May Christ be with you as you write.

For Parents:

This letter is a chance to say some things that don't often get put into words. Your parenting job is coming to an end with your love. Let this letter be an occasion to say what these years of loving him/her have meant to you, to put your love into words.

Let the letter also be an occasion to express the faith that has been a foundation for your love. They know it from having lived with you, but hearing it will add a new stimulus for their own developing faith and it will open up a whole new possibility of growing in faith together, of adult-to-adult sharing.

And if this day has prompted any ideas about how you on your part could help the relationship with your son/daughter, some new gift of yourself to him/her, that also could be included in a letter.

Enjoy the writing. May Christ be with you as you write.

(Contributed by Robert Doolittle, Reading, Massachusetts)

MOTHERS DAY RHYME

Here's a fun little presentation that your kids could put on for their mothers on Mothers Day, or anytime they want to honor their moms. Each kid carries in a large placard with one of the letters M-O-T-H-E-R on it, and recites a verse.

M is for my muddy feet
That tracked across the floor,
All the many, many times
I slammed the kitchen door.

Those days are gone forever,
My footprints you'll not see,
Especially if I'm slippin' in
At twenty-five 'til three.

O is for orange juice and oatmeal,
I've spilled upon my clothes;
And aren't you glad, dear mother,
You no longer wipe my nose?

I'll clean my room, set the table,
My efforts will deserve a star,
I'll even hang up all my clothes,
If you'll let me have the car.

There's lots of words that start with T,
About my childhood days,
Like Tinker-toys and tooting trains,
And temperatures and trays.

You need not worry and fret now
When I'm feeling not my best,
I'm really not so sick, you know,
I'm only facing tests.

H is for her loving heart,
And a hug and gentle hand
That shaped a lot of hamburgers
And dumped a lot of sand. . .

From tennis shoes and pockets,
She combed it from my hair,
I'll need help again, I'm sure,
As long as the beach is there.

(E) Each day I'm grateful for her help
For everything she's done,
To help me shape up as I should
And be a perfect son.

I've given up lots of habits,
I'd rather not say which,
In case I try them just once more
Before I find my niche.

(R) "Really? Really? Really!"
Her frustration sometimes shows.
But she comes through, with colors true,
As everybody knows.

She puts up with lots of things,
I know that it's a chore,
I'll try not to ask for favors,
If she'll drive me to school *once* more.

(Contributed by Anne Hughes, Dickinson, Texas)

PARENT'S PERSPECTIVE

Lead the youth group in a discussion using the questions below. Begin by welcoming them to the meeting as if they were their parents. Without actually being told what is happening, the kids will catch on pretty fast. Tell them that you want to discuss a few issues that concern them and their teenage children. Allow the group to respond as if they were their parents. You may have to remind them now and then who they are. At the conclusion of the discussion, have the kids check out Ephesians 6:1-3, and discuss what it means to them (as kids).

Discussion Questions:

1. What would you do if someone you loved very much refused to accept or return your love?
2. How do you communicate with someone who answers every question with "Yes," "No," or "I don't know" or with a shrug?
3. How do you free someone who has depended on you for life itself, particularly when you fear that he is going to make some bad choices and get hurt?
4. Where do you get all the money it takes every year to support a child?
5. What would be your reaction if your child always valued his friend's opinions and ignored yours?
6. What would you do if your child regularly disobeyed you?
7. How would you feel if your child outwardly rejected the things that are most important to you?

(Contributed by Chuck Williams, Bryan, Texas)

PARENT SWAPPING

Here's an idea that may take a little advance planning, but the results are worth the effort. Have the kids in your group switch families for a weekend to see what it is like to live with someone else's parents. Then on Sunday, when the experience is over, discuss feelings and impressions that the teens had about their experiences. Some sample questions for discussion:

1. Did you think that the parents treated you just like they treat their own kids?
2. What rules did you have to obey that are not put into practice at your own home?
3. Was it hard to get along with other brothers and sisters?
4. Did you act differently than you would have acted had you been at home?
5. What benefits did you get from the experience?

There are lots of other questions that the kids can discuss, of course, and you might even conduct a similar discussion with the parents. (Contributed by Donna McElrath, Upper Marlborough, Maryland)

PARENT YOUTH GROUP

For one evening, day or weekend, do with the parents of the kids in your group what you would normally do with the kids. Play the kids' favorite games, sing the songs they like best, conduct a discussion, do a skit, or anything else that you would do with the youth group on a typical day. At the end of the time ask the parents to answer these questions:

1. What are the good and poor things you notice about the group?
2. What would you like to see happen in the future?
3. How can we better help your son or daughter?
4. How can we better serve your family?

It is a good idea to meet periodically with parents anyway, and this is a good way to let them know exactly what is going on with their kids and the youth group. (Contributed by Alva J. Wiersma, Englewood, Colorado)

STAY AT HOME WEEK

Perhaps your church can organize a "Stay-at-home" Week for families of the congregation. Too often, when a church tries to minister to families, it winds up scheduling more meetings that only prevent families from staying home and being families. Something like a "Stay-at-home" Week would have to be introduced early enough so that every family could plan to set the week aside and to participate fully.

The basic idea is to provide families with both the motivation and the resources to do things together as a family for the entire week. After the week-long experience, families could share at a church service how it went for them. The purpose is to hopefully get something started, so that families will continue doing similar things together on their own.

One church that conducted a "Stay-at-home" Week for their families printed up a program for the week that each family was to follow. It provided suggestions for family activities, but allowed each family's own flexibility and creativity. Here is a summary of the week-long program that was printed up and distributed to the families.

Monday
Theme: The Family

Begin your "Stay At Home Week" today by calling your family together and deciding when, each day, you can all spend time together in recreation, Bible study, and worship. Some suggestions for a family meeting time are:

• after the evening meal before leaving the table
• a half hour before putting the children to bed
• a half hour early each morning before going to work or school

A Guide for Tonight's Devotions.

Ask questions of each family member concerning your family, such as:

A. What is a family?
B. What is a family for?
C. Do we need a family?
D. What would it be like without a family?
E. Who instituted the first family?

Scripture Reading.

Read out loud and from two translations, the second chapter of the book of Genesis.

Some Conclusions You May Draw from the Scripture Reading.

A. God instituted and ordained the family unit.
B. Marriage and the family unit is God's plan for men and women.
C. In the family, one should find, Love, Purpose, Acceptance, Peace, and Happiness.
D. The family is as important to God today as it was when He first formed it.

Close With Prayer.

You may want to have sentence prayers or have a different family member lead in prayer each night.

Tuesday
Theme: What Love Is . . .

Suggested Activity.

How long has it been since your family has looked at your Family Picture Album or past vacation pictures? How about pulling those out tonight and reminiscing over those great times you have had together as a family? Happy browsing!

Scripture Reading.

Read I Corinthians 13 from the King James and a New English Version or The Living Bible if possible.

Guide for Tonight's Devotions.

Discuss verses 4-7. Tell how each family member can work toward this perfect love. Memorize by repeating, "Love never stops." I Cor. 13:8; and, "Through love, help one another," Gal. 5:13.

Conclusions.

Love is the greatest of the three spiritual gifts which last forever. We are commanded by God to first love the Lord with our total being, then love our fellowman as much as we love ourselves. This includes our own family members. Evaluate your love on the basis of patience, kindness, unselfishness and consistency. Only God can give us the love described in I Cor. 13:4-7. Strive for this perfect love. Be grateful for the love in your home.

Wednesday
Theme: Family Worship and Service

This evening is a time to spend in worship with your family. Here is an outline of a service your family can participate in. You will find time for scriptures, songs, prayer and discussion. Don't worry about how it all sounds, particularly the singing. God listens to our hearts, not just our voices. Let everyone take a part in the worship service.

SCRIPTURE: Psalm 37:3-6

SONG: (Provide words to one or two songs here)

PRAYER: Pray for God's leadership in the worship time.

SCRIPTURE: Ephesians 4:11-16 (Modern paraphrase, if possible). Discuss again the important role of each family member in the light of this scripture. Also discuss what God expects of each family member. (Eph. 5-6:1)

SONG: (Provide words to another familiar song)

SCRIPTURE: (Provide a selection of scriptures here that can be read as a responsive reading by family members)

PRAYER: Pray that your family will be bound together by God's love in service to Him, that as a family, you will be Holy, for He is Holy.

SONG: (Provide words to another closing song)

Thursday
Theme: Bible Games

Children learn Bible truths through Bible games. Parents can too. Choose two or more of these activities to do.

1. **Complete the verses:**
    A. And the Lord God said, It is not _____ that _____ should be _____. Genesis 2:18
    B. _____ thy _____ and thy _____, as the Lord thy God hath _____ thee. Deu. 5:16
    C. Let us not love in _____, neither in _____, but in _____ and in _____. I John 3:18
    D. Even a _____ is known by his _____. Prov. 20:11
    E. Have _____ one with another. Mark 9:50

II. **Unscramble these verses:**
    A. love as shalt thyself Thou neighbor thy. Mark 12:31
    B. parents this right Children for your obey the is in Lord. Eph. 6:1
    C. kind ye another to Be one. Eph. 4:32
    D. answer grievous wrath soft anger but away a stir words us turneth. Prov. 15:1
    E. good Lord unto He give is for the O thanks. Psalm 118:1

III. Divide into two teams and play **Charades** or **Who Am I?** with clues about Bible characters and events.

IV. **Alphabet Game:** The first one names a word related to a Christian family beginning with letter A, the next repeats that word then adds a word beginning with letter B, and so forth.

V. **For preschoolers:** Draw pictures of family group. These persons are important to you. They are also important to God and to many other people.

Conclude with a prayer of thanksgiving and sing together the song . . . (provide words to a familiar chorus)

Friday
Theme: Family Fun and Recreation

Tonight can be a real time of fun together.

Why not . . .

A. Have a cookout
B. Play some family oriented games either inside or out.
C. Plan some special treat for the children.
D. Go to a ball game together.

Just enjoy being together and having fun as a family.

Saturday
Theme: Family Work and Commitment

This day can be a workday for the family, working together on a project around the house. Try to find a job that can be finished today.

Time should be spent evaluating the week's activities. What have you gained this week as a "family?" What have you gained as an "Individual?"

Joshua 24 should be read (the entire chapter) with special emphasis on verse 15. Discuss the application of the account in Joshua 24 to your family's spiritual life. Spend time in prayer, with each family member dedicating themselves to serving the Lord, as a family. Pray also that God will use your family in a special way to serve Him, that your family might be an example for others to follow.

Sunday
Theme: The Family at Church

How long has it been since your whole family has sat together at church? Today you have an opportunity to worship the Lord together as a family unit. As God has blessed you this past week, give praise and thanks to Him for your family. Pray not only for your family, but for the family in general that, with God's leadership, it will remain strong.

(Contributed by Elene Harger, Lubbock, Texas)